MW00988343

AI from a Black Guy

Wofford, Jeffrey E. - Author

AI from a Black Guy / Wofford, Jeffrey

Includes biological references and index.

ISBN: 9798872359241

1. Business/Entrepreneurship
2. Artificial Intelligence (AI)

Edited by: Nathan D. Cruise

Cover design by: Jeffrey E. Wofford

January 15, 2024

AI FROM A BLACK GUY

TABLE OF CONTENT

Preface

AI from a Black Guy: Navigating the Future – Insights and Resource Guide" is more than a journey through the realms of Artificial Intelligence (AI); it's a beacon of empowerment and inclusivity in a field that has long been dominated by a homogeneous perspective. This guide seeks to illuminate the path for underrepresented communities, including Black, Hispanic, Women, LGBTQ, and other minority groups, showcasing how AI can be a tool for transformative change and innovation.

Central to this mission is BlackPowerAI.com, a pivotal resource intricately interwoven throughout this guide. BlackPowerAI.com is not just a website; it's a gateway to empowerment in the AI space. The platform serves as a one-stop resource for those looking to carve their niche in the AI-driven entrepreneurial world. This platform provides users with AI website creation tools, domain names, digital marketing, and resources needed to create and build their own AI enterprises, thus democratizing access to technology and entrepreneurship.

Moreover, BlackPowerAI.com is connected to the Wofford Excellerate Group, an AI consulting firm that offers expertise and support for developing AI ideas into viable business solutions. This linkage ensures that users not only have access to technological tools but also to professional guidance and consultancy, bridging the gap between concept and execution.

The importance of BlackPowerAI.com in the broader context of this guide cannot be overstated. It stands as a practical embodiment of the book's core message: that AI is for everyone, and its potential can be fully realized only when diverse voices contribute to its development and application. The website offers an array of resources, including books, educational materials, and links to community networks, that can help users get started on their AI journey.

As we navigate through the various chapters of "AI from a Black Guy," keep in mind BlackPowerAI.com as a dynamic resource. Whether you're a student, entrepreneur, professional, or simply an AI enthusiast, this website, alongside our guide, provides a comprehensive foundation for understanding AI and harnessing its power for entrepreneurial and societal advancement.

In conclusion, "AI from a Black Guy: Navigating the Future – Insights and Resource Guide," together with BlackPowerAI.com, represents a synergistic effort to foster diversity, equity, and inclusion in the AI landscape. They serve as a testament to the power of AI as a tool for positive change and a call to action for underrepresented communities to claim their space in this exciting and evolving field.

Chapter 1 – The Origins and Pioneers of AI

A Journey Through Time

Embark on a philosophical odyssey as we unravel the ancient riddles that hinted at the unthinkable—crafting machines with cognitive abilities. In the realms of Aristotelian inquiry, the profound dialogues of Aristotle himself beckon us to contemplate whether entities beyond the biological realm could replicate the soul itself and reasoning.

In the sacred halls of ancient philosophy, Aristotle, a luminary of intellectual exploration, sparked dialogues that reverberated through the corridors of time. His inquiries into the nature of the soul, consciousness, and reasoning laid the groundwork for profound contemplation on the essence of being. As we journey through these inquiries, we confront the age-old questions that Aristotle pondered, which echo into the realm of crafting intelligent machines.

Aristotle's exploration of the faculties of the soul, encompassing reason, perception, and intellect, becomes a guiding light in our journey. Once deemed exclusive to living organisms, these faculties now beckon us to contemplate whether the essence of intelligence can be in a robot or non-biological mechanism.

The heart of our odyssey lies in the audacious question—can we replicate the sublime art of reasoning, a pinnacle of human cognition, in entities that transcend the confines of the organic? The contemplation of this question opens gateways to a future where machines possess not just computational power but the ethereal quality of reasoning.

As we journey through time, guided by the intellectual torchbearer Aristotle, we wear the unthinkable. The once-mythical concept of machines endowed with cognitive abilities becomes a tangible prospect, challenging the very core of our understanding of consciousness, reason, and the soul.

Our exploration extends beyond philosophy to tangible examples in history and modernity. From ancient automata and mythical creations to contemporary artificial intelligence, we witness the echoes of the Aristotelian inquiry manifest in our quest to create machines with cognitive prowess.

We bridge the ancient and the modern, contemplating the profound questions that have guided humanity's intellectual evolution. In synthesizing philosophy and technological advancement, we unveil the threads that weave the fabric of crafting cognitive machines. This journey transcends the ages and beckons us to redefine the very essence of what it means to be intelligent.

Plato's Cave Allegory: A Journey into Perception and Reality

Plato's Cave Allegory, found in Book VII of "The Republic," is a profound exploration of human perception, reality, and the transformative power of knowledge. In this allegory, prisoners are chained inside a dark cave, facing a wall where shadows flicker from a fire behind them. These shadows are the prisoners' only perception of the external world. One day, a prisoner is freed and exposed to the world outside the cave, illuminated by the sun. The freed prisoner experiences a radical shift in perception, realizing the shadows were mere illusions and a higher reality exists outside the cave.

The shadows stand for the illusions and misconceptions that individuals accept as reality. In the context of modern discussions on artificial intelligence, the shadows can symbolize the limited understanding or biased perspectives that AI might develop based on incomplete or skewed data.

The chains symbolize societal constraints, traditions, or preconceived notions that limit individuals from questioning their perceived reality. Similarly, the "chains" could represent the limitations imposed by biased algorithms or narrow datasets in AI.

The freed prisoner's journey into the sunlight symbolizes the philosopher's ascent to knowledge and enlightenment. In the context of AI, it could represent the evolution of AI systems from narrow, shadowy perceptions to broader, more informed understandings through continuous learning and exposure to diverse data.

The allegory includes the freed prisoner's return to the cave to rescue others. In this example, the philosopher has to share knowledge and insights. In the AI domain, it could represent the responsibility of those involved in AI development to rectify biases and share transparent, ethical practices.

Plato associates the sun with the Form of the Good, the ultimate source of truth and knowledge. In AI discussions, this can be analogous to the ethical frameworks and guiding principles that should illuminate the development and application of AI technologies.

Imagine an AI system trained on limited datasets that perpetuate stereotypes. The "freedom" here would involve recognizing and rectifying these biases, allowing the AI to see a more accurate representation of the world.

Limited Data Perspectives

An AI system focused on a narrow dataset may have a distorted perception of reality. Exposing it to a more extensive and diverse dataset would be akin to bringing it out of the cave, broadening its understanding.

The allegory can inspire AI developers to "ascend" to ethical considerations, ensuring that their creations contribute positively to society and don't perpetuate harmful illusions.

In delving into Plato's Cave Allegory, we find a timeless exploration of the transformative power of knowledge and the continuous journey to perceive a more profound reality—themes that echo in contemporary discussions on artificial intelligence and its potential to shape our understanding of the world.

Plato's Cave AI Parallels

Plato's Cave Allegory, nestled in the pages of "The Republic," invites us into a profound philosophical odyssey, where prisoners confined in a cave perceive shadows as their reality. Let's unravel this allegory and draw parallels to the world of artificial intelligence:

In AI, shadows could represent biased algorithms, where the system perceives a skewed reality based on incomplete or prejudiced data.

The chains symbolize constraints in the form of biased training data or narrow algorithmic pathways that limit the AI's understanding.

Understanding one's exposure to sunlight mirrors the AI's evolution from narrow, biased perspectives to broader, enlightened understandings through continuous learning.

The return to the cave is akin to the responsibility in AI development to rectify biases, share insights, and uphold ethical practices.

The sun symbolizes ethical frameworks and transparency in AI
development, illuminating the path toward responsible AI.

Venturing back to ancient Greece, we encounter early experiments in crafting artificial entities, or automata:

The marvels of ancient Greece found resonance in the AI domain through early attempts to create artificial life, analogous to the AI community's fascination with crafting intelligent entities.

- Examples:
    - In ancient Greece, inventors crafted water clocks with automaton figurines. Today's AI can be seen as a sophisticated evolution, measuring, and interpreting time in ways unimaginable in antiquity.
    - The Antikythera Mechanism is an ancient Greek analog computer used to predict astronomical positions. This mechanism parallels the modern AI system's ability to predict complex patterns and trends.

In Summary: This dual exploration takes us from the shadows of perception in Plato's Cave to the nascent stirrings of artificial life in ancient Greece. It's a timeless journey where philosophical contemplation converges with early experiments in crafting intelligent entities—a narrative that resonates in ancient and contemporary landscapes.

Chinese Automata

Take a journey to ancient China, where inventors dabbled in creating automata. These early experiments, often imbued with cultural and mystical significance, offer a glimpse into the cross-cultural tapestry of early artificial intelligence endeavors.

As we traverse the landscapes of ancient philosophy and witness the birth pangs of automata, we unveil the primordial chapters in the saga of artificial intelligence. This journey through time sets the stage for the myriad innovations and challenges that lie ahead in our exploration of the AI landscape.

In the enchanting landscape of ancient Greece, inventors delved into the realm of crafting artificial life through ingenious automata. Let's embark on a comparison and contrast, focusing on the remarkable creations of Heron of Alexandria.

Automata: A Glimpse into Ancient Ingenuity

- **Contrast in Purpose**

    - Comparison: Both ancient and modern automata aim to replicate life.
    - Contrast: Ancient automata often served as entertainment or religious artifacts, while modern counterparts span various applications, including industry and AI.

The Intricacy of Mechanisms

- Comparison: Both share intricacy in design.
- Contrast: Ancient automata were mechanically driven and relied on gears and simple mechanisms. Modern AI involves complex algorithms, machine learning, and neural networks.

- Comparison: Automation is central to both.
- Contrast: Ancient automata had predefined movements, while modern AI adapts and learns dynamically based on data.

Examples:

- o Mechanized scenes depicting mythological tales, showcasing ancient Greece's artistry and mechanical prowess.
- o A modern marvel where AI algorithms and sensors automate the complex task of driving, adapting to real-time conditions.

- Comparison: Both reflect the cultural and philosophical underpinnings of their times.
- Contrast: Ancient automata often held religious or mythological significance, while modern AI reflects societal advancements and ethical considerations.

In comparing Heron's automata to contemporary AI, we witness the evolution from mechanically driven marvels to dynamic learning systems. While ancient automata stood as testaments to craftsmanship and mythological storytelling, modern AI permeates diverse facets of our lives, transforming industries and shaping the future. It's a journey where the essence of crafting artificial life echoes through the corridors of time.

Ancient Marvel: The Antikythera Mechanism

- **Advanced Technology:** The Antikythera Mechanism, discovered in a shipwreck, astounds with its analog precision. A device believed to predict astronomical positions reflects advanced technological insight in ancient Greece.

- **Philosophical Implications:** The mechanism showcases technological prowess and raises questions about the depth of ancient understanding of celestial mechanics and the cosmos.

- **Ingenious Chinese Automata:** Unveiling Automation in Ancient China.

- **Early Automation:** Beyond the Mediterranean, ancient China delved into automation, showcasing early attempts to create artificial entities.

- **Philosophical Embedment:** The creations held practical significance and embedded philosophical notions, reflecting Chinese perspectives on life and nature.

- **Yan Shi's Automaton:** A Human-Like Creation in Ancient China.

- **Human Resemblance:** Yan Shi, a legendary figure, is said to have crafted an automaton resembling a human, blurring the lines between natural and artificial.

- **Philosophical Sparks:** The creation of human-like entities prompted philosophical discussions about the essence of life and the boundaries between the natural and the artificial.

Key Insights:

Both the Antikythera Mechanism and Chinese automata reveal a shared pursuit of technological excellence in diverse ancient cultures.

The Antikythera Mechanism and Chinese automata intersect in their capacity to spark philosophical discussions about the cosmos or the nature of life.

The critical insight highlights that the foundations of Artificial Intelligence are rooted not only in technological innovations but also in the musings and creative endeavors of ancient civilizations.

The convergence of ancient Greek and Chinese ingenuity laid the groundwork for the extraordinary journey into the evolution of AI, with early aspirations manifesting in mechanical marvels.

Dr. Timnit Gebru - Forging Black Excellence in AI

As we look at Pioneers of AI, Dr. Timnit Gebru emerges as a luminary, transcending the conventional boundaries of technology to carve a path steeped in ethics and inclusivity. This chapter unveils the profound journey of a visionary, born and raised in Ethiopia, who served as a Research Scientist in Google's Ethical AI Team but also pioneered the transformative initiative, Black in AI.

Championing Ethical AI

Dr. Gebru's TED Talks stand as beacons, illuminating the way forward for ethical AI. With a focus on preventing marginalization, her insights delve into the nuanced realm of AI limitations. Her commitment to ensuring the just and equitable use of artificial intelligence positions her as a leading advocate for ethical considerations in the ever-evolving technology landscape.

Founding Black in AI

The genesis of Black in AI echoes the personal experience of Dr. Gebru as the lone Black figure in AI conferences. Fueled by a desire to rectify this lack of representation, she embarked on a mission to create change. What began as a Facebook group evolved into a global initiative, Black in AI, serving as a nexus for Black professionals in AI to connect, collaborate, and elevate the collective presence of Black individuals in the field.

Addressing the Diversity Gap: Dr. Gebru's advocacy extends beyond her corporate role, actively confronting the stark diversity gap, particularly the underrepresentation of Black women in AI. Black in AI is not merely an organization; it's a dynamic community fostering inclusivity. Its initiatives inspire the next generation of Black professionals, breaking down barriers and inviting them into the vibrant world of technology.

- **Corporate Sponsorships and Travel Grants:** The impact of Black in AI reverberates beyond virtual connections. Dr. Gebru and her team have successfully secured corporate sponsorships, translating into tangible support through travel grants. This strategic move not only fosters networking opportunities but physically places Black professionals at pivotal conferences, disrupting conventional norms and challenging the status quo.

- **Encouraging Future Generations:** At the heart of Dr. Gebru's advocacy lies a profound commitment to inspiring Black youth to envision themselves in the tech industry. Her TED Talks serve as powerful testimonials, urging those with an interest in research, engineering, and AI to embark on meaningful careers. This chapter unfolds not just as a celebration of one individual's achievements but as a catalyst for a broader ripple effect, shaping the future of AI inclusivity.

As we navigate this exploration, we celebrate Dr. Timnit Gebru as a trailblazer, a visionary weaving a narrative of inclusivity and equity in the tapestry of AI. Her contributions resonate as a clarion call for a more diverse and equitable future in the realm of artificial intelligence.

AI History from a Black Guy

In crafting the narrative of "AI from a Black Guy," we venture into the compelling histories that laid the foundation for artificial intelligence. This chapter, "Pioneering the Path," invites readers to explore the revolutionary ideas of Alan Turing and the collaborative genius of Warren McCulloch and Walter Pitts.

Alan Turing: The Trailblazer

Alan Turing's brilliance transcends his cryptographic triumphs during World War II. We delve into his visionary mind, unveiling the universal computing machine's role in shaping our understanding of computational limits. Turing's intellectual odyssey, computability to breaking the Enigma code, becomes a testament to his indomitable spirit.

The Turing Test, a concept questioning machine intelligence's boundaries, takes center stage. The Imitation Game, a defining moment, challenges readers to ponder the essence of intelligence and its manifestation in machines.

McCulloch and Pitts: Architects of Artificial Neurons

Warren McCulloch, the neurophysiologist, and Walter Pitts, the logician, form an intellectual partnership that reshapes the AI landscape. Their collaboration introduces artificial neurons, laying the groundwork for neural network models.

As we explore their journey, we encounter the translation of biological neuron functionality into logical constructs. The McCulloch-Pitts Neuron Model emerges as a pivotal breakthrough, providing a simplified yet profound representation of biological neurons.

Connecting the Dots: A Key Insight

These narratives converge to illuminate a central theme: Alan Turing's visionary ideas, notably the Turing Test, become the bedrock for envisioning machine intelligence. Simultaneously, the collaboration between McCulloch and Pitts introduces logical neurons, an elemental force propelling the evolution of neural networks. "Pioneering the Path" becomes a chapter that echoes the resilience and innovation defining the history of AI.

Ada Lovelace's Vision

In the annals of AI history, the often-overlooked contributions of Ada Lovelace shine as a beacon of foresight. Long before the advent of modern computing, Lovelace envisioned machines not merely as calculators but as entities capable of manipulating symbols. Her prescient insights laid the groundwork for understanding that machines could extend beyond numerical tasks, foreseeing the expansive realm of AI applications.

Diving into Lovelace's visionary writings, we uncover her conceptualization of machines generating not only numbers but also symbolic operations. As we illuminate this forgotten chapter, readers will gain a profound appreciation for Lovelace's role as a trailblazer in the expansive landscape of artificial intelligence.

George Boole's Algebraic Logic

The journey through the forgotten vanguards of AI takes us to the mathematical brilliance of George Boole. His groundbreaking work in algebraic logic becomes a cornerstone in creating algorithms, a linchpin in the development of artificial intelligence.

Explore how Boole's systematic approach to logical reasoning provided the theoretical framework for constructing algorithms. Unraveling the intricacies of Boole's algebraic logic, we discover its profound impact on the very essence of AI—transforming logical operations into a language machine could comprehend.

As we delve into the narratives of Ada Lovelace and George Boole, "Beyond the Blueprint" emerges as a chapter and as a tapestry woven with forgotten vanguards' insights. Ada Lovelace's vision and George Boole's algebraic logic intertwine to showcase the diverse threads that form the fabric of artificial intelligence's rich history.

Conclude this enlightening journey through the history of AI by reflecting on the legacy of innovation left by diverse minds. Explore the profound impact that contributors from various backgrounds and perspectives have had on shaping AI into the dynamic and transformative field it is today. This section encourages readers to appreciate the richness and depth of the narratives often overlooked, emphasizing that innovation in AI has been a collective endeavor.

Shift the focus towards the future, underlining the critical importance of inclusivity for the continuous advancement of AI. Discuss the role of this inclusivity in inspiring the next generation of innovators, engineers, and thinkers. Highlight initiatives and strategies that aim to create pathways for diverse talents to contribute to and lead future developments in AI. The chapter concludes by laying down a call to action, inviting readers to be active participants in shaping an innovative AI landscape and representative of the diversity inherent in our global society.

In essence, this chapter is more than a historical narrative; it's a testament to the diversity of thought and the collaborative spirit that propels the field of AI forward. Reflecting on the past and inspiring the future aligns seamlessly with the overarching theme of "AI for a Black Guy," emphasizing the celebration of AI history and advocating for inclusivity as the driving force for its future.

Chapter 2 - Understanding AI and its Business Applications

What Is Artificial Intelligence?

Artificial Intelligence refers to developing computer systems that can perform tasks that typically require human intelligence. These tasks encompass a broad spectrum, including problem-solving, learning from experience, understanding natural language, recognizing patterns, and making decisions. In essence, AI systems simulate human cognitive functions, enabling machines to perform tasks that, until recently, only humans could accomplish.

AI systems are designed to:

- Reason: AI systems can analyze information, draw conclusions, and decide based on available data.

- Learn: AI can improve its performance on a specific task by learning from data and experience.

- Perceive: AI systems can interpret and understand various forms of data, such as images, text, and sound.

- Interact: AI systems can engage in natural language conversations, interacting with users in a human-like manner.

AI is categorized into two main types: Narrow AI (also known as Weak AI) and General AI (also known as Strong AI)

- Narrow AI refers to AI systems designed and trained for a specific or limited range of tasks. These systems excel in
- performing well-defined functions, such as language translation, image recognition, or playing chess. However, they need to gain the general intelligence and adaptability of humans.

- General AI, on the other hand, represents a level of artificial intelligence that can understand, learn, and apply knowledge across various tasks, much like a human being. This level of AI, often portrayed in science fiction, has the potential to reason, learn, and adapt in ways that go beyond predefined functions.

Currently, Narrow AI is the predominant form of AI in use, while achieving General AI remains a long-term goal of AI research.

AI vs. Traditional Software

It is essential to differentiate AI from traditional software. Traditional software operates based on explicit instructions written by programmers. It follows a set of predefined rules to perform specific tasks. In contrast, AI systems learn and adapt from data, allowing them to improve their performance over time without explicit programming.

- **Key Differences:**
    - Flexibility: Traditional software is rigid and designed for specific tasks, while AI systems can adapt to new situations and learn from data.
    - Rule-Based vs. Data-Driven: Traditional software relies on predefined rules, while AI uses data and algorithms to make decisions.

Automation: AI can automate tasks that require human-like intelligence, making it suitable for complex, dynamic environments.

The AI Landscape

Opportunities and Challenges

The AI landscape is brimming with opportunities and challenges for individuals, businesses, and society. As AI technologies advance, they unlock new possibilities across various domains:

- **Business Optimization:** AI streamlines operations, enhances customer experiences, and improves business decision-making, increasing efficiency and profitability.

- **Healthcare Advancements:** AI aids in disease diagnosis, drug discovery, and personalized medicine, potentially revolutionizing healthcare delivery.

- **Autonomous Systems:** AI powers autonomous vehicles, drones, and robots, enabling safer, more efficient transportation and manufacturing.

- **Natural Language Understanding:** AI-driven language models like ChatGPT improve human-computer interactions, making AI more accessible and user-friendly.
- **Environmental Impact:** AI contributes to ecological monitoring, climate modeling, and sustainable practices, addressing critical global challenges.

However, the widespread adoption of AI also raises concerns, including ethical considerations, job displacement, data privacy, and algorithmic bias. As we delve deeper into the AI landscape, we will explore these opportunities and challenges in more detail, offering insights into how AI leadership can help navigate this complex terrain.

In the following section, we will delve deeper into the world of AI, exploring its practical applications, ethical considerations, and the strategic role of AI leadership in driving success. So, let's embark on this journey of discovery, where AI's potential knows no bounds, and its impact on businesses and society continues to unfold.

The AI Game-Changer

Artificial intelligence (AI) has emerged as a game-changer in today's rapidly evolving business landscape. This chapter delves into the profound impact of AI on businesses across various industries. From practical applications and real-world success stories to its role in gaining a competitive advantage and driving digital transformation, we explore how AI reshapes the business world.

AI Applications Across Industries

AI is not limited to a single industry, its transformative potential spans many sectors. Here, we'll delve into some of the key industries where AI is making a significant impact:

- **Healthcare:** AI is revolutionizing patient care through predictive analytics, image analysis, and drug discovery, improving diagnostic accuracy and patient outcomes.

- **Finance:** In the financial sector, AI is employed for fraud detection, algorithmic trading, credit scoring, and customer service, enhancing operational efficiency and risk management.

- **Retail:** AI-driven recommendation systems, inventory optimization, and supply chain management drive personalized shopping experiences and boost sales.

- **Manufacturing:** AI-powered robotics and automation optimize production processes, reduce downtime, and ensure product quality.

- **Customer Service:** Chatbots and virtual assistants transform customer interactions, provide round-the-clock support, and improve customer satisfaction.
- **Transportation:** AI plays a crucial role in autonomous vehicles, optimizing traffic management and enhancing logistics and delivery services.
- **Energy:** AI is used for predictive maintenance of equipment, optimizing energy consumption, and improving the efficiency of renewable energy sources.

Business AI Success

The business world is replete with compelling AI success stories. Companies that have embraced AI technologies are reaping the benefits. Here are a few notable examples:

- **Netflix:** The streaming giant uses AI algorithms to analyze user data and recommend personalized content, resulting in more prolonged viewer engagement.

- **Amazon:** AI-driven logistics and supply chain management have allowed Amazon to optimize its delivery processes, reducing shipping times and costs.

- **Tesla:** Tesla's self-driving cars utilize AI for real-time navigation, making autonomous driving a reality.

- **IBM Watson:** IBM's Watson AI platform assists in healthcare research, helping clinicians analyze patient data to make more informed treatment decisions.

AI's Impact on Competitive Advantage

AI has become a potent tool for gaining a competitive edge. Businesses that harness AI technologies can:

- **Enhance Decision-Making:** AI-driven insights enable data-driven decision-making, leading to more informed and strategic choices.
- **Personalize Customer Experiences:** AI-powered personalization improves customer engagement, retention, and satisfaction.
- **Optimize Operations:** AI automates processes, streamlines operations, and reduces costs, improving efficiency and productivity.

- **Innovate Products and Services:** AI enables the development of innovative products and services that cater to evolving customer needs.

AI and Digital Transformation

Digital transformation, integrating digital technologies into all aspects of a business, is driven by AI. AI is the linchpin of this transformation, offering the ability to:

- **Automate Manual Processes:** AI automates repetitive tasks, freeing up human resources for more creative and strategic endeavors.

- **Leverage Big Data:** AI can analyze vast datasets, extract valuable insights, and drive data-driven strategies.

- **Enhance Customer Engagement:** AI-powered chatbots and virtual assistants provide personalized customer interactions at a scale.
- **Improve Predictive Capabilities:** AI's predictive analytics help businesses forecast trends, customer behavior, and market dynamics.

As AI continues to evolve, its role in digital transformation becomes increasingly vital. The chapters will explore how AI leadership can drive and navigate these transformative changes, ensuring businesses stay competitive and innovative in an AI-driven world.

The HUMANE AI Pin

A real-life view on understanding AI and Business is HUMANE. HUMANE the Company encapsulates a holistic philosophy that reshapes how technology interacts with our daily lives. Key pillars include:

Human-Centric: HUMANE prioritizes human needs and experiences over purely technical or commercial considerations. It seeks to enhance the quality of life by aligning technology with genuine user needs.

- **User-Friendly:** The user experience is central to HUMANE, emphasizing intuitive design, ease of use, and accessibility. Complex technologies are simplified to ensure broad inclusivity.

- **Mindful:** HUMANE promotes mindful interactions with technology. It encourages awareness of the impact of digital experiences on mental health, productivity, and overall well-being.

- **Ethical:** At its core, HUMANE stands for ethical technology. It upholds principles such as transparency, user autonomy, and data privacy, ensuring that technology serves humanity without exploitation.

For Those Who Have HUMANE Technology:

- **Enhanced Well-Being:** Users experience technology as a positive force in their lives, contributing to mental and emotional well-being.

- **Empowerment:** Individuals feel empower

ed to make informed decisions, with a sense of control over their digital experiences.

- **Inclusivity:** HUMANE design ensures that technology is accessible to diverse groups, promoting inclusivity and reducing digital divides.

For Those Who Have Not Yet Experienced HUMANE Technology:

- **Potential Disadvantages:** Individuals may miss out on the positive impact of user-centric and ethical tech practices.

- **Privacy Concerns:** Without HUMANE principles, there may be heightened risks of privacy breaches and exploitation of user data.

- **Limited Empowerment:** Users may feel less in control of their digital experiences, facing challenges related to transparency and autonomy.

This section provides a foundational understanding of HUMANE Corporation AI Pin technology, outlining its principles and exploring how it impacts the daily lives of those who have embraced it and those who have not yet experienced its benefits.

Ethical Foundations of HUMANE

- **Ethical Tech Principles:** Transparency: HUMANE is built on the principle of transparency, ensuring that users understand how technology operates, how data is used, and the implications of their interactions.

- **User Autonomy:** Central to HUMANE is the recognition of user autonomy, empowering individuals to make informed decisions about their digital interactions without coercion or manipulation.

- **Data Privacy:** HUMANE places a strong emphasis on safeguarding data privacy, employing robust measures to protect user information from unauthorized access or misuse.

Contrast with Past Practices:

Shift from Exploitation to Empowerment: In the past, some technologies were designed to exploit user data for profit without adequate transparency. HUMANE represents a paradigm shift by prioritizing user empowerment over-exploitation.

- **User-Centric Design:** Unlike previous practices that prioritized business interests, HUMANE puts users at the center, focusing on designing technologies that serve their needs while respecting ethical boundaries.
- **Inclusive Decision-Making:** HUMANE seeks to include diverse voices in the decision-making process, avoiding biases present in earlier technologies that disproportionately affected certain groups.

Compelling Examples:

- **Algorithmic Transparency:** HUMANE-driven platforms provide users with insights into how algorithms make decisions, ensuring transparency in processes like content recommendation or job application screenings.

- **Privacy-Centric Features:** HUMANE-designed applications prioritize privacy features, such as end-to-end encryption in messaging apps or anonymous browsing modes, respecting user confidentiality.

- **User-Driven Customization:** Unlike past practices of pushing content for profit, HUMANE platforms offer users customization options, allowing them to shape their digital experience according to personal preferences.

This section highlights the ethical underpinnings of HUMANE technology and the Company, showcasing its departure from exploitative practices and providing examples that demonstrate a commitment to transparency, user autonomy, and data privacy.☐

Chapter 3 – Developing AI Strategy and Building Teams

The Executive's Responsibility in AI

As businesses embrace AI, the role of leadership in navigating this transformative journey becomes paramount. In this chapter, we delve into the executive's responsibilities in AI, the importance of fostering an AI-ready culture, the central role of data, and the critical considerations of ethics, bias, and responsibility.

The adoption and integration of AI technologies require active involvement from top leadership. Executives bear several crucial responsibilities in driving AI initiatives:

- **Setting the Vision:** Executives must define the strategic vision for AI within the organization, outlining how it aligns with broader business goals and objectives.

- **Allocating Resources:** Adequate resources, both financial and human, should be given to support AI initiatives, including research, development, and implementation.

- **Risk Management:** Identifying and mitigating risks associated with AI, including data privacy, security, and ethical concerns, is a core responsibility.

- **Building the Right Team:** Executives should assemble a team with the skills and expertise to execute AI projects effectively.

Building an AI-Ready Culture

Creating a culture that embraces AI is pivotal for success. An AI-ready culture is characterized by:

- **Continuous Learning:** Encouraging employees to acquire AI-related skills and stay updated on AI advancements.

- **Innovation:** Fostering an environment that encourages experimentation and innovation with AI technologies.

- **Data-Driven Decision-Making**: Promoting the use of data and analytics for informed decision-making at all levels of the organization.

- **Collaboration:** Facilitating cross-functional partnerships to harness the collective intelligence of the workforce are tenets for suggestion.

The Role of Data in AI Leadership

Data is the lifeblood of AI, and its effective management is fundamental to AI leadership. Critical aspects of data in AI leadership include:

- **Data Strategy:** Developing a clear data strategy that outlines data collection, storage, quality assurance, and utilization.

- **Data Governance:** Implementing robust data governance practices to ensure data integrity, security, and compliance.

- **Data Monetization:** Exploring opportunities to monetize data assets, potentially creating new revenue streams.

- **Data Ethics:** Ethical considerations in data usage, including privacy, consent, and transparency, must be integrated into the data strategy.

Ethical considerations take center stage as AI becomes more integrated into business processes. AI can inadvertently perpetuate biases present in training data. Therefore, executives must:

- **Ensure Ethical AI:** Set clear ethical guidelines for AI development and deployment, prioritizing fairness, transparency, and accountability.

- **Address Bias:** Implement mechanisms to identify and rectify biases in AI algorithms and decision-making processes.
- **Regulatory Compliance:** Stay informed about evolving AI regulations and ensure compliance to avoid legal and reputational risks.
- **Responsible AI:** Embrace a culture of responsible AI use, acknowledging the potential societal impact of AI technologies.

In the following chapters, we will delve deeper into these facets of AI leadership and guiding.

Using AI to Win!

In the previous chapters, we've explored the fundamental aspects of AI and its transformative potential. Now, it's time to delve into the practicalities of crafting a comprehensive AI strategy. This chapter will guide you through defining your AI vision and goals, aligning your AI strategy with your broader business objectives, developing a roadmap for AI adoption, and efficiently allocating resources and budgets to support your AI initiatives.

Defining Your AI Vision and Goals

Consider how AI can enhance your organization's operations, products, or services. Think about the unique value AI can bring to your industry.

- **Goal Setting:** Set clear, measurable goals for your AI initiatives. These include improving operational efficiency, enhancing customer experiences, or launching AI-driven products.

- **Long-Term Vision:** Consider the long-term impact of AI. How will AI evolve within your organization over the next five, ten, or twenty years?

Aligning AI Strategy with Business Goals

- **Business-First Approach:** The business AI strategy should align with the broader strategy. AI should serve as an enabler of your business objectives.

- **Cross-functional collaboration:** Involve key stakeholders from various departments in developing your AI strategy. Collaboration fosters a shared understanding of AI's role in achieving business goals.

- **Risk Assessment:** Evaluate the potential risks and challenges of your AI initiatives and develop mitigation strategies.

Developing a Roadmap for AI Adoption

- **Phased Approach:** Divide your AI journey into manageable phases. Start with pilot projects to gain experience and build confidence.

- **Technology Stack:** Identify the AI technologies and tools that align with your strategy. Consider factors such as scalability, integration capabilities, and vendor partnerships.

- **Data Strategy:** Outline how you will collect, store, and leverage data to fuel your AI initiatives. Data is the lifeblood of AI.

- **Talent Acquisition:** Assess your organization's AI talent needs and develop a plan for recruitment, training, or partnerships to fill skill gaps.

Budgeting and Resource Allocation for AI

- **Financial Planning:** Determine the financial resources required for your AI strategy, which includes technology investments, talent costs, and ongoing maintenance.

- **ROI Analysis:** Conduct a thorough return on investment (ROI) analysis to understand the expected benefits of AI adoption. Finances will help justify the budget allocation.

- **Scalability:** Consider how your AI initiatives will scale over time. Be prepared to allocate additional resources as your AI capabilities grow.

- **Monitoring and Optimization:** Allocate resources for continuous monitoring and optimization of AI systems. AI is dynamic, and regular improvements are essential.

By the end of this chapter, you will have the foundational knowledge and tools to craft a robust AI strategy that aligns with your organization's vision, supports its business objectives, and ensures efficient resource allocation. The journey to AI leadership is exciting and transformative; a well-defined strategy is your compass for success.

AI Talent and Teams

As you embark on your journey to AI leadership, it's imperative to understand that the success of your AI initiatives largely depends on the talent and teams you assemble. This chapter will explore the critical aspects of building and managing AI teams, including key roles and skills, talent acquisition and retention strategies, leveraging external AI expertise, and fostering a collaborative environment conducive to AI innovation.

Key Roles and Skills:

- **AI Leadership:** Identify leaders who can champion AI initiatives within your organization. They should possess a deep understanding of AI's strategic value and be able to guide its implementation.

- **Data Scientists:** Data scientists are the architects of AI models. They should have data analysis, machine learning, and statistical modeling expertise.

- **Machine Learning Engineers:** These professionals design and implement machine learning algorithms. They bridge the gap between data science and software engineering.

- **AI Ethicists:** As AI raises ethical concerns, having experts in AI ethics is crucial. They ensure responsible AI development and deployment.

- **AI Product Managers:** AI product managers translate business goals into AI solutions. They bridge the gap between technical and non-technical stakeholders.

- **Recruitment Strategy:** Develop a comprehensive strategy for recruiting AI talent. Strategies may include partnerships with universities, attending AI conferences, or leveraging AI job boards.

- **Competitive Compensation**: Offer competitive salaries and benefits to attract and retain AI professionals. AI talent is in high demand.

- **Continuous Learning:** Encourage ongoing learning and development within your AI teams. Recruiting. Support certifications and courses to keep skills current.

- **Diversity and Inclusion:** Foster a diverse and inclusive workplace. Various teams often lead to more creative and effective AI solutions.

Leveraging External AI Expertise

- **Consultants and Contractors:** Consider hiring AI consultants or contractors for specific projects or expertise gaps. They can provide valuable insights and accelerate project timelines.

- **Academic Collaborations:** Collaborate with universities and research institutions to tap into cutting-edge AI research and emerging talent.

- **AI Service Providers:** Leverage AI service providers for cloud-based AI solutions or AI-as-a-service offerings.

Fostering a Collaborative Environment

- **Cross-Functional Teams:** Encourage collaboration between AI teams and other departments like marketing, operations, and sales. AI integration into various aspects of your organization.

- **Communication:** Establish open communication channels to facilitate knowledge sharing and idea exchange between AI teams and non-technical stakeholders.

- **Innovation Culture:** Cultivate an organizational culture that values experimentation and embraces the iterative nature of AI development.

- **Agile Practices:** Implement agile methodologies to enable rapid AI prototyping and deployment.

By the end of this chapter, you will have a comprehensive understanding of how to build, nurture, and manage AI talent and teams. As AI becomes increasingly central to your organization's success, investing in the right people and fostering a collaborative culture will be critical to achieving your AI leadership goals.

Chapter 4 - Data Management for AI

The Critical Role of Data

In artificial intelligence (AI), data is the lifeblood that fuels innovation and drives insights. This chapter delves into the critical role of data in AI leadership, emphasizing the significance of data collection, quality, management, privacy, and compliance.

Data as a Strategic Asset

In the contemporary digital landscape, data isn't merely a byproduct; it's a strategic asset that, when harnessed effectively, can catapult organizations and influencers to unprecedented heights. Integrating website and social media data within ecosystems magnifies the significance of this invaluable asset.

- **Data Amalgamation:** A Holistic View Imagine a company operating a standalone website and managing social media profiles on various platforms without data capture. Each platform generates data – website analytics, Facebook likes, Twitter retweets, and Instagram comments. These disparate data streams, when integrated, provide a holistic view of audience behavior.

  o Example 1: Unifying User Engagement Metrics A company's website might attract substantial traffic but likes and shares on social media platforms reflect a different facet of audience engagement. Integrating these metrics offers a unified perspective. For instance, if a product page on the website sees high traffic but needs more social media shares, it suggests a potential gap in social promotion.

o Example 2: Cross-Platform Audience Insights Consider an influencer managing a blog, YouTube channel, and Instagram account. Integrating data from these platforms unveils cross-channel insights. If the blog audience predominantly engages with long-form content, crafting similar content for YouTube could resonate. This cross-platform analysis is a data-driven strategy derived from an integrated ecosystem.

- **Strategic Decision-Making:** Integrated data is more than just amassing information and leveraging insights for informed decision-making.

o Example 3: Tailoring Content Strategies A company notices a spike in website traffic following a successful Instagram campaign. Integrated data allows for a deeper dive – understanding which Instagram posts drove traffic. Armed with this knowledge, the company can tailor future content strategies, ensuring alignment with what resonates most with the audience.

o Example 4: Personalized Marketing Campaigns For an influencer, integrated data can unveil audience demographics across platforms. Knowing that a significant portion of the audience engages during evenings on Instagram informs when to schedule posts or launch live sessions, enhancing the impact of personalized marketing campaigns.

Shaping Future Endeavors

Data, when harnessed strategically, becomes a compass for shaping the future.

- o Example 5: Product Development Integrated data reveals what content resonates and what audience preferences. A company can extrapolate this to inform product development – creating offerings that align with the tastes and preferences of its audience, thus reducing the risk associated with new ventures.

- o Example 6: Predictive Analytics As data accumulates within the integrated ecosystem, predictive analytics powered by AI can forecast trends. For instance, understanding seasonal shifts in engagement patterns enables proactive content planning, ensuring timely and relevant communication.

Integrating website and social media data transforms these datasets from isolated fragments into strategic assets. It's not just about knowing; it's about understanding, interpreting, and using that understanding to chart a course toward future success.

Data-Driven Decision-Making

Embrace a data-driven decision-making culture where AI insights guide your strategic choices, product development, and customer interactions.

- **Unstructured Data:** Recognize the value of unstructured data, including text, images, audio, and video, in generating valuable insights and innovation.

Data Collection and Quality Management

The journey begins with data in the vast landscape of artificial intelligence. It's not just about gathering volumes of information but strategically selecting the correct data that harmonizes with your AI strategy and business goals. For instance, a healthcare AI project aiming to enhance patient outcomes may prioritize collecting data on patient demographics, medical history, and treatment efficacy.

- **Prioritizing patient outcomes:** This ensures that the data collected aligns with the specific objectives of the AI initiative, enhancing its relevance and impact.

- **Data Quality Assurance:** The foundation of any robust AI system lies in its data quality. As a chef selects the finest ingredients for a masterpiece, data quality assurance involves meticulous cleaning, validation, and enrichment techniques. Imagine an e-commerce AI that recommends products to users based on their preferences.

The recommendations could be off-target if the underlying data needs more accurate and complete information. Data quality assurance acts as the culinary expertise, ensuring that the AI algorithms work with a dataset that is reliable, accurate, and conducive to producing valuable insights.

- **Governance:** Data governance is the framework that upholds your data's integrity, security, and compliance. The guardian ensures your data remains consistent, protected, and aligned with regulatory standards. Consider a financial institution implementing AI for fraud detection.

Data governance would manage practices, how customer financial data is handled, who has access to it, and how it complies with financial regulations. This proactive approach safeguards sensitive information and builds trust in the AI system's ethical use of data.

- **Data Lifecycle Management:** The data lifecycle mirrors the natural course of existence, from birth to eventual renewal. In the context of AI, it spans data acquisition, storage, usage, and even disposal. Responsible data lifecycle management acknowledges the importance of each stage.

    o For example, an environmental AI tracking carbon emissions might gather real-time data from various sources, store it securely, and periodically archive older datasets. Responsible data lifecycle management optimizes resource usage and adheres to sustainability goals, emphasizing that responsible management from inception to expiration is paramount, even in the digital realm.

Data Privacy and Compliance

- **Navigating Data Privacy Regulations:** Discuss the evolving landscape of data privacy regulations (e.g., GDPR, CCPA) and their implications for AI projects.

- **Ethical Considerations:** Explore the moral dimensions of AI data usage, addressing issues of bias, fairness, and transparency.

- **Security Measures:** Highlight the importance of robust cybersecurity measures to protect sensitive data from breaches and unauthorized access.

- **Compliance Frameworks:** Provide an overview of compliance frameworks and certifications relevant to AI, such as ISO 27001 and SOC 2.

By mastering the nuances of data in the context of managed AI data compliance measures, compliance platforms will be better equipped to harness its power and make informed, strategic decisions that drive AI initiatives and business success.

Collecting the Right Data: Strategic Alignment for AI Success

- **Understanding Relevance:** Collecting data is not just about quantity but strategic alignment. The first step in this journey is identifying and gathering data that directly aligns with your AI strategy and broader business objectives.

  o Example 1: Personalized Marketing An e-commerce platform aiming for personalized marketing focuses on collecting customer browsing behavior, purchase history, and social media interactions. This ensures the data collected is directly relevant to enhancing the customer experience through targeted campaigns.

- **Strategic Relevance for AI:** The collected data must serve the strategic goals for AI's effectiveness. Relevant data empowers machine learning models to make informed predictions and decisions. It's not just about having data; it's about having the correct data.

- **Analytics to social media:** interactions, empowers decision-makers with a comprehensive view of audience behaviors and preferences.

  o Example 2: Informed Content Creation Imagine a media house integrated across platforms. Insights from website analytics reveal the topics resonating with the audience.

  o Example 3: Predictive Maintenance in Manufacturing In manufacturing, collecting real-time data from machinery provides the relevant inputs for an AI-driven predictive maintenance system. This aligns with the strategic goal of reducing downtime and optimizing operational efficiency.

Data Quality Assurance: The Pillars of Reliable Data

- **Data Cleaning:** Maintaining high data quality starts with data cleaning. This involves identifying and rectifying errors or inconsistencies in the dataset. Clean data ensures the accuracy of AI models and the reliability of subsequent analyses.

    o Example 4: Customer Database Cleanup A financial institution periodically conducts data cleaning on its customer database. This involves correcting inaccuracies in names, addresses, and contact information. The result is a more reliable dataset for AI applications like credit scoring.

- **Validation Techniques:** Data validation is an ongoing process to ensure that incoming data meets specific criteria or standards. Implementing validation techniques adds a layer of reliability to the data collected.

  o Example 5: Healthcare Data Validation In healthcare, data validation techniques are crucial. For patient records, validation checks ensure that critical information, such as diagnosis codes and treatment details, meets established standards for accuracy.

- **Enrichment for Enhanced:** Insights: Data enrichment involves enhancing existing data with additional information. This can include appending demographic details, socio-economic indicators, or other relevant data points.

  o Example 6: Sales Leads Enrichment A sales-focused organization enriches its leads data with additional information about company size, industry, and recent news. This enhanced dataset provides a more comprehensive view of AI-powered lead scoring.

Data Governance: Ensuring Consistency and Compliance

- **Establishing Policies:** Data governance involves setting up policies and procedures for data management. This includes defining who has access to the data, how it's used, and ensuring compliance with relevant regulations.

- o Example 7: Financial Data Governance In the financial sector, data governance policies dictate who can access sensitive financial transaction data. This ensures that customer financial information is handled securely and complies with industry regulations.

- **Security Measures:** Data governance also addresses data security concerns. This includes implementing measures to protect against uninsured access to data breaches and ensuring the confidentiality of sensitive information.

  - o Example 8: Secure Handling of Personal Information An e-commerce platform implements data governance measures to secure personal information such as credit card details. This involves encryption, access controls, and regular audits to ensure compliance with data protection laws.

Data Lifecycle Management: Responsible Stewardship

- **Acquisition and Storage:** Data lifecycle management begins with the acquisition of data. It involves thoughtful storage strategies, considering volume, velocity, and variety.

  - o Example 9: Big Data Storage Strategies An organization dealing with big data adopts scalable storage solutions to accommodate the vast amount of data generated. This includes cloud-based storage and distributed file systems for efficient data handling.

- **Archival and Disposal:** Responsible data management extends to archival and disposal. Archiving preserves valuable data for historical reference, while disposal ensures that irrelevant or outdated data is safely removed.

  o Example 10: Archiving Research Data In a research institution, data lifecycle management includes archiving research datasets. This archival process ensures that valuable scientific data is preserved for future reference.

- **Environmental Considerations:** The responsible disposal of data involves considerations for ecological impact. This can include securely wiping electronic data or responsibly destroying physical records.

  o Example 11: Eco-Friendly Data Disposal. A technology company adopts eco-friendly practices for data disposal, ensuring that electronic components are recycled responsibly and that paper records are shredded for recycling.

In conclusion, effective data collection, quality assurance, governance, and lifecycle management are pillars of a robust data strategy. When these aspects are thoughtfully addressed, organizations lay the foundation for AI success, ensuring that the data powering their intelligent systems is abundant, reliable, secure, and aligned with strategic goals.

Chapter 5 – AI in Practice

The AI Symphony

In the ever-evolving landscape of digital ecosystems, Artificial Intelligence (AI) emerges as the master conductor, orchestrating a harmonious symphony from the raw notes of integrated data. This section delves into the transformative role of AI in gleaning actionable insights, predicting trends, and automating digital marketing strategies.

Predictive Analytics

AI elevates predictive analytics to unprecedented heights by discerning patterns and extrapolating future trends from integrated data.

- o Example 1: Forecasting Content Trends Consider a media company with a website, YouTube channel, and social media presence. Analyzing integrated data, AI identifies content themes that historically triggered engagement spikes. Predictive analytics can then forecast upcoming trends, enabling the company to create content aligned with anticipated audience preferences proactively.

- o Example 2: Anticipating Product Demand: AI can predict product demand for an e-commerce business, integrating website transactions and social media interactions. By analyzing past data, it identifies products likely to trend. The company can strategically stock inventory, ensuring readiness to meet anticipated surges in demand.

Personalized Recommendations

AI's capacity to understand individual preferences transforms the user experience by offering personalized recommendations.

- o Example 3: Tailored Content Suggestions In a content-rich ecosystem, such as an online magazine with articles, videos, and social media snippets, AI can curate personalized content suggestions. If users frequently engage with technology-related articles, AI ensures their feed is rich with such content, enhancing user satisfaction and retention.

- o Example 4: Precision Marketing Offers AI can craft personalized marketing offers for an e-commerce platform integrated with customer data from various touchpoints. If a customer consistently explores a particular product category, AI can automate targeted promotions, enhancing the likelihood of conversion.

Automating Digital Marketing Strategies

AI becomes the engine driving automated, data-driven digital marketing campaigns.

- o Example 5: Dynamic Ad Campaigns Imagine an advertising campaign that dynamically adjusts content based on user preferences. Analyzing integrated data in real-time, AI ensures that users see the most relevant aspects of a product or service, maximizing engagement and conversion rates.

- o Example 6: Adaptive Social Media Scheduling For an influencer managing multiple platforms, AI can automate social media scheduling. By understanding when the audience is most active across integrated platforms, AI ensures content goes live optimally, enhancing reach and engagement.

The Future Landscape

The future of digital ecosystems lies in a seamless integration of AI, transforming data into insights and actions.

- o Example 7: Autonomous Marketing Strategies As AI evolves, it promises autonomous marketing. Integrated data feeds into AI systems that predict trends and autonomously execute marketing strategies, adapting to shifting audience behaviors in real-time.

In conclusion, AI emerges as the linchpin in integrating website and social media ecosystems. It's not merely a tool; it's the visionary force propelling digital strategies into a future where data isn't just interpreted; it's intelligently utilized to chart a course toward unparalleled success.

Data as an Asset: Unlock the Power Within

In the contemporary business landscape, data is not merely a byproduct but a strategic asset of immense value. The understanding and utilization of data go beyond mere operational insights; it forms the cornerstone of gaining a competitive edge. Let us delve into the intricacies of this pivotal concept.

Understanding Data Beyond Operation

Data is often generated at every touchpoint of a business operation, from customer interactions on a website to social media engagements. Recognizing that this Data holds inherent value beyond its immediate operational context is the first step in harnessing its strategic potential.

- Example 1: Customer Journey Insights

  Consider an e-commerce platform tracking customer interactions on its website. Instead of merely seeing this data as a record of transactions, analytical thinkers recognize it as a treasure trove of insights into the customer journey. Analyzing patterns can reveal preferences, pain points, and opportunities for enhancement.

Competitive Advantage Through Strategic Utilization

Strategic assets are those that, when effectively harnessed, provide a competitive advantage. In the realm of data, it's about moving beyond reactive analysis to proactive utilization. This involves using data to understand past performance and predict and shape future outcomes.

o   Example 2: Predictive Analytics in Retail

A retail chain strategically employs predictive analytics on integrated data from its website, social media, and in-store transactions. This anticipates customer preferences and optimizes inventory, ensuring the right products are stocked at the right time. The result is a competitive edge in meeting customer demands.

Strategic Decision-Making

Its role in decision-making is at the heart of data as a strategic asset. Strategic decision-makers leverage data to inform choices that align with organizational goals and market trends. It's about transforming raw data into actionable insights that steer the ship in the right direction.

o   Example 3: Market Expansion Strategy

A tech company eyeing international markets strategically utilizes data on website traffic, social media engagement, and global market trends. This informs a market expansion strategy tailored to the unique demands of different regions, demonstrating how data guides pivotal decisions.

Futureproofing Through Data

Strategic assets are those that not only provide an advantage today but also futureproof the organization. When viewed as a strategic asset, data becomes a tool for adapting to evolving market dynamics and eventually staying ahead.

- o Example 4: Adapting to Industry Trends

Adapting to Industry Trends

It is leveraging Data as a Strategic Asset. In the dynamic media realm, staying ahead isn't just about keeping up with current audience preferences; it's about anticipating the next wave of content consumption patterns. For a forward-thinking media company, data isn't a mere record of the past; it's a crystal ball into the future.

This proactive stance toward data marks a shift in perspective, a recognition of its inherent value beyond historical documentation. Treating data as a strategic asset transforms organizations from passive collectors into architects of their destiny, leveraging the power within their data assets for sustained success.

The journey begins with the understanding that data is not a static entity but a living, breathing force that pulses with insights. Through advanced analytics, a media company amalgamates data, discerns upcoming trends, and crafts personalized recommendations. It's not just about data-driven decisions; it's about data-inspired innovation.

In this transformed landscape, the media company isn't merely pushing content; it's engaging in a nuanced conversation with its audience. The data-driven approach doesn't just ensure relevance; it creates an experience that feels tailor-made for each individual. It's about offering what the audience wants now and predicting what they'll crave next.

Imagine a scenario where the company's data infrastructure operates like an autonomous navigator, adjusting marketing strategies in real-time. This isn't a shot in the dark; it's a calculated dance with data, a harmonious rhythm that resonates with the ever-evolving preferences of the audience.

The power of data as a strategic asset lies not just in its historical value but in its ability to guide decisions, predict trends, and foster an ongoing dialogue with the audience. It's not a one-size-fits-all approach; it's a dynamic orchestration, a symphony of personalized content that speaks to each viewer.

For media companies embracing this paradigm shift, data isn't a puzzle to be solved; it's a treasure trove waiting to be unlocked. By treating data as a strategic asset, these organizations position themselves as spectators and active participants in the ever-changing landscape of the media industry.

As we gaze upon this tapestry of digital innovation, we see a landscape transformed. The integration of website ecosystems, driven by consolidated likes and follows, is not a mere evolution but a revolution in how we understand, interact with, and leverage the digital sphere.

- o Example 5: Autonomous Digital Ecosystems In the future, we envisage digital ecosystems that operate autonomously. At the helm, AI interprets integrated data in real-time, adjusts strategies, and offers experiences with minimal human intervention. The result is a dynamic, responsive, and ever-evolving digital landscape.

The integration of website ecosystems, portrayed in our exploration, is not just a convergence of platforms; it's a celebration of the interconnectedness that defines the digital era. It is a journey into a future where data isn't just integrated; it's intelligently utilized, creating a symphony of digital innovation that resonates with the unique preferences of each participant. As we step into this future, the tapestry we have woven serves as a testament to the boundless possibilities at the intersection of technology, data, and human experience.

Conclusion: A Tapestry of Digital Innovation

As we draw the curtain on this chapter, we paint a vibrant vision of the future where the integration of website ecosystems transcends strategic necessity to become the heartbeat of digital innovation. This concluding section weaves together the threads of our exploration, showcasing how a tapestry of interconnected platforms, fueled by consolidated likes and follows, signifies a strategic choice and a transformative journey into a more insightful, personalized, and AI-driven digital landscape.

Insightful Decision-Making

Integrating website ecosystems lays the foundation for insightful decision-making—amalgamating diverse data sources from website feedback. Decision-makers can strategically guide content creation, aligning it with audience preferences to ensure maximum impact.

Personalized User Experiences

This integration not only informs decisions but elevates user experiences to unprecedented heights. Consolidated data allows for personalized interactions, ensuring users are met with content and offerings tailored to their preferences.

- o Example 6: Seamless User Journeys For an e-commerce platform integrating website and social media data, a user navigating through products on the website seamlessly finds tailored recommendations on their social media feed. The integration ensures a consistent and personalized journey, fostering user satisfaction and loyalty.

AI-Infused Possibilities

Crucially, this tapestry is embroidered with the intricate patterns of Artificial Intelligence. The integrated data becomes the palette from which AI draws, crafting predictive analytics, personalized recommendations, and automated digital marketing strategies.

Executing Your AI Strategy

In this section, we delve into the practical aspects of bringing your AI strategy to life. Implementation is where your AI vision transforms into tangible solutions. We explore the processes, best practices, and challenges involved in implementing AI effectively.

Prototyping and Experimentation

- **The Power of Prototyping:** Prototyping in the realm of AI is akin to sketching the blueprint before constructing a building. This section unpacks the transformative potential of building AI prototypes. By creating tangible, scaled-down versions of AI solutions, businesses can validate concepts, identify potential pitfalls, and refine their approach. The power lies not just in envisioning but in tangibly experiencing the AI solution's functionality, fostering a deeper understanding that goes beyond theoretical discussions.

Agile and Iterative Development

Agility and iteration form the backbone of successful AI development. This part of the chapter introduces the concept of agile methodologies applied to AI. Unlike traditional, linear development, agile emphasizes flexibility, rapid iteration, and continuous improvement. The iterative nature allows for adjustments based on real-time feedback, ensuring that AI solutions evolve in tandem with changing requirements and insights. It's about fostering a culture where adaptation is not an exception but a norm, ensuring that the AI journey is a responsive, dynamic, and continuously improving process.

The AI Development Lifecycle

- **Phases of AI Development:** Embarking on an AI journey
  involves traversing distinct phases. This section navigates
  through the comprehensive AI development lifecycle. It starts
  with defining the problem at hand, progresses through
  meticulous data collection, ventures into the intricate realm of
  model training, orchestrates deployment strategies, and
  culminates in vigilant monitoring. By breaking down the journey
  into these phases, organizations gain a roadmap for structured
  and effective AI development. Each phase brings its unique
  challenges and considerations and understanding them is
  paramount for a successful AI implementation.

- **AI Development Tools:** Tools are the artisans' instruments in
  the realm of AI development. This part of the chapter introduces
  the diverse array of tools and frameworks that have become the
  backbone of AI development. From the powerhouse TensorFlow
  to the flexibility of PyTorch and the simplicity of scikit-learn,
  these tools empower developers and data scientists to sculpt and
  refine AI solutions. Each tool has its strengths, and
  understanding when and how to wield them is akin to mastering
  the palette for an artist. This exploration ensures that
  organizations are not just equipped with AI ambitions but also
  armed with the right tools to bring those ambitions to life.

Managing AI Projects: Best Practices

- **Project Management for AI:** Effective project management is
  the backbone of successful AI endeavors. This section delves
  into the best practices that underpin managing AI projects. From
  crystallizing clear objectives to meticulously defining roles and

responsibilities, and establishing realistic project timelines, these practices form the scaffolding that supports the entire AI project lifecycle. The intricacies of AI development require a robust project management framework, ensuring that teams are aligned, resources are optimized, and objectives are achieved with precision.

- **Cross-Functional Teams:** In the landscape of AI, diversity in expertise is a cornerstone. This part of the chapter illuminates the significance of assembling cross-functional teams. These teams, comprising data scientists, engineers, domain experts, and business leaders, bring a spectrum of perspectives and skills to the table. The synergy of these diverse minds is essential for navigating the multifaceted challenges that AI projects often present. By fostering collaboration across disciplines, organizations can harness the full spectrum of talent required to steer AI projects to success.

- **Effective Communication:** Communication is the lifeblood of any project, and in the realm of AI, where technical intricacies meet business objectives, it becomes paramount. This segment underscores the critical role of effective communication in AI project success. It goes beyond technical jargon, ensuring that insights and progress are conveyed in a manner understandable to both technical and non-technical stakeholders. By fostering a culture of transparent and clear communication, organizations can bridge the gap between AI teams and the wider business context, aligning everyone toward common goals.

- **Data Challenges:** Navigating the complexities of data is a central theme in AI implementation. This section meticulously addresses common data-related challenges that organizations encounter, such as data scarcity, data labeling intricacies, and concerns related to data privacy. Furthermore, it provides strategies and methodologies to surmount these challenges, ensuring that the foundational element of AI—data—is robust, reliable, and ethically handled throughout the implementation process.

- **Model Bias and Fairness:** Addressing the ethical dimensions of AI, this part of the chapter illuminates the challenges associated with model bias and fairness in AI systems. It delves into the complexities of ensuring that AI models are not inadvertently biased and that they exhibit fairness in their predictions and outcomes. The chapter provides insights into detecting and mitigating biases, offering a roadmap for organizations to foster fairness and ethical considerations in their AI implementations.

- **Scalability and Performance:** Scalability is a critical consideration as AI solutions evolve. This segment explores the considerations for scaling AI solutions to handle larger datasets and increased workloads. It delves into the intricacies of ensuring that AI implementations can seamlessly adapt to growing demands without compromising performance. By understanding the nuances of scalability, organizations can future-proof their AI solutions and ensure they remain performant in dynamic environments.

- **Regulatory Compliance:** In the labyrinth of AI implementation, navigating regulatory landscapes is paramount. This section underscores the importance of adhering to regulatory and ethical guidelines throughout the AI implementation process. It explores the intricacies of compliance, providing insights into the frameworks and standards that govern AI applications. By prioritizing regulatory compliance, organizations can ensure that their AI implementations align with legal and ethical standards, mitigating risks and fostering trust.

Conclusion: Navigating the AI Implementation Odyssey

The journey of implementing AI is undoubtedly a challenging odyssey, fraught with complexities that demand careful consideration and strategic finesse. As we traverse the landscape of overcoming implementation challenges, several key takeaways emerge.

Holistic Data Management: The bedrock of AI, data, demands meticulous management. Overcoming challenges related to data scarcity, labeling intricacies, and privacy concerns requires a holistic approach. Organizations must prioritize robust data practices, ensuring reliability, ethical handling, and a commitment to privacy.

- **Ethical Compass in AI:** In the ethical realm, addressing model bias and ensuring fairness is imperative. The takeaway is a clarion call for organizations to embed ethical considerations into the DNA of their AI implementations. Detecting and mitigating biases are not just technical endeavors but ethical imperatives.

- **Future-Ready Scalability:** The scalability of AI solutions is non-negotiable in a dynamic landscape. Understanding the nuances of scalability prepares organizations for the future, ensuring that AI implementations can seamlessly adapt to evolving datasets and increasing workloads.

- **Guided by Regulatory North Stars:** Amidst the technological prowess, regulatory compliance stands tall. Navigating the regulatory landscape is not just a legal necessity but a fundamental aspect of responsible AI. The takeaway is a reminder that adherence to regulations is not a hurdle but a guiding North Star, ensuring that AI implementations align with legal and ethical standards.

Trust as the True North

Ultimately, the overarching theme is trust. Overcoming implementation challenges is not just about technical adeptness; it's about fostering trust. Trust in data quality, trust in ethical considerations, trust in scalability and trust in regulatory adherence. As organizations embark on their AI implementation journeys, trust becomes the true north, guiding them through challenges toward the realization of AI's transformative potential.

Harmonious AI Alignment

In the dynamic landscape of AI, understanding the impact of initiatives is paramount. This chapter is a compass for organizations seeking not just to deploy AI but to measure and amplify its influence, ensuring a harmonious alignment with strategic objectives.

- Selecting Meaningful KPIs: Navigating the Metrics Landscape

  Embarking on the journey to measure AI impact begins with choosing the right metrics. Consider a scenario where a retail giant deploys AI to enhance customer experience. The meaningful KPIs here extend beyond sales figures; they include customer satisfaction scores, click-through rates, and perhaps even social media sentiment analysis. By exploring this process, you gain insights into how to choose KPIs that truly reflect the transformative power of AI in your unique context.

- Types of AI KPIs: Unveiling the Rich Tapestry

  The chapter unfolds various categories of AI KPIs, akin to exploring different hues of impact on a canvas. Picture a scenario in a healthcare setting where AI is employed to streamline patient care. Outcome-based KPIs go beyond the financial realm and delve into patient recovery rates, reduce hospitalization times, and improve overall well-being. Simultaneously, process-based KPIs, such as the accuracy of diagnostic models, become pivotal. This exploration demystifies the landscape of AI KPIs, empowering you to harness the richness of impact measurement effectively.

- Example: In the healthcare scenario, the deployment of AI resulted not just in reduced costs but, more importantly, in a tangible improvement in patient recovery rates—a testament to the profound impact on human lives.

The Measurement Framework: Navigating the AI Landscape

Think of a measurement framework as the blueprint for your AI impact assessment. It's the GPS that guides you through the intricacies of data collection, reporting tools, and data analysis techniques. Imagine a scenario where an e-commerce giant adopts AI for personalized recommendations. The framework, in this context, involves tracking user interactions, employing analytics tools, and utilizing machine learning models to understand customer preferences. This exploration equips you with the knowledge to design a comprehensive measurement framework tailored to your AI endeavors.

- Example: Through a robust measurement framework, the e-commerce giant identified that personalized recommendations not only increased user engagement but also significantly boosted sales, showcasing the tangible impact of AI on business metrics.

Data-Driven Decision Making: Steering AI with Informed Choices

Data is the fuel that powers the engine of AI. Emphasizing the importance of data-driven decision-making is like teaching the driver how to navigate and control the vehicle. Picture an AI-powered marketing campaign where data on customer preferences directs the content and timing of promotional materials. This section underscores how decisions informed by data analysis can optimize

AI performance. It's not just about having data; it's about using it strategically to refine and improve your AI initiatives.

- Example: In the marketing campaign, data-driven decision-making revealed that adjusting the timing of promotional emails based on customer behavior led to a significant increase in click-through rates, demonstrating the pivotal role of informed choices in AI impact.

In the dynamic landscape of AI, data serves as the compass, guiding strategic decisions that propel initiatives forward. Comparable to a skilled driver navigating a vehicle, data-driven decision-making forms the bedrock of effective AI utilization. Imagine an AI-driven marketing campaign fine-tuned by insights into customer preferences. This section illuminates the transformative power of informed choices in optimizing AI performance. It's not merely about possessing data; it's about strategically deploying it to elevate and refine AI endeavors. The example of adjusting email timing based on data-driven insights in a marketing campaign vividly illustrates the profound impact of judicious decision-making on AI outcomes, underlining the strategic synergy between data and AI success.

AI Continuous Learning

In the dynamic landscape of AI, understanding the impact of initiatives is paramount. This chapter is a compass for organizations seeking not just to deploy AI but to measure and amplify its influence, ensuring a harmonious alignment with strategic objectives.

Sustaining AI Excellence

Continuous monitoring is akin to having a vigilant guardian for your AI systems, ensuring they remain accurate, efficient, and compliant amidst the ever-changing business landscape. Imagine an AI-driven chatbot for customer support; continuous monitoring involves tracking its interactions to guarantee it consistently provides helpful and contextually relevant responses. This section delves into the significance of ongoing vigilance to uphold AI excellence.

- Example: In the case of the chatbot, continuous monitoring identified patterns in customer queries, allowing for real-time adjustments to enhance response accuracy and overall user satisfaction

Feedback Loops: The Iterative Path to Improvement

Feedback loops in AI systems are like the iterative loops in a creative process. They enable adaptive learning and refinement, ensuring that AI models evolve with changing dynamics. Picture an AI-powered recommendation engine for an online streaming service. Feedback loops involve analyzing user reactions to suggested content, refining the model based on preferences, and creating an ever-improving cycle. This exploration sheds light on how feedback loops drive continuous improvement in AI systems.

- Example: The streaming service, through feedback loops, discovered that users appreciated recommendations aligned with their viewing habits, leading to a refined model that significantly increased user engagement.

Demonstrating ROI

Calculating AI ROI is akin to the foundational step of any journey— understanding your starting point and the distance traveled. It involves methodologies that delve into the quantitative and qualitative factors contributing to the Return on Investment (ROI). Picture a scenario where AI is implemented to streamline customer service; ROI calculations extend beyond cost reductions to include improved customer satisfaction scores and reduced resolution times. This section presents the methodologies to navigate the numbers game of AI impact.

- Example: For the customer service AI implementation, calculating ROI includes not just the reduction in service costs but also the increase in customer satisfaction, providing a holistic view of the investment's impact.

Communicating AI Value: The Art of Expression

Communicating AI value is akin to narrating a compelling story. It involves strategies for effectively conveying the transformative power of AI to executives, stakeholders, and the broader organization. Imagine you're presenting the impact of an AI-driven predictive maintenance system; effective communication here involves not just raw performance metrics but also narratives of avoided downtimes and increased operational efficiency. This exploration unfolds strategies for the artful expression of AI's value.

- **Example:** In presenting the predictive maintenance system, effective communication involves not only stating increased efficiency but also telling stories of how it prevented critical equipment failures, showcasing the tangible value brought by AI.

Measuring AI Impact – Summary

In the dynamic terrain of artificial intelligence, comprehending the impact of initiatives stands as a cornerstone for organizations. This chapter serves as a guiding compass, not merely for those deploying AI but for those aiming to measure and magnify its influence. The imperative is clear: understanding AI's resonance is vital for steering the course in alignment with strategic objectives. As organizations delve into the metrics, frameworks, and communication strategies, they gain not just an assessment tool but a powerful instrument to amplify the transformative force of AI. This journey ensures that the true essence of AI, its impact, is not only measured but also communicated, fostering a harmonious integration into the strategic fabric of the organization.

☐

AI Security and Ethics

In the ever-evolving landscape of artificial intelligence, safeguarding the integrity and ethical use of AI systems is non-negotiable. This chapter serves as a guardian, addressing the paramount importance of fortifying AI against potential risks and ensuring its ethical deployment.

Embarking on the exploration of AI security demands an understanding of the potential threats that lurk in the digital shadows. Picture an e-commerce giant employing AI to enhance customer recommendations. The security risks extend beyond traditional concerns and encompass data breaches, where sensitive customer information becomes a target. Additionally, adversarial attacks — attempts to manipulate the AI model's decision-making — and vulnerabilities in the model itself add layers of complexity. This exploration unravels the various dimensions of AI security risks, offering a comprehensive map of the digital battlefield.

As knights armed with ethical considerations, organizations must not merely respond to security challenges but anticipate and prevent them. Consider the concept of "ethical by design," akin to forging a shield that encompasses ethical considerations throughout the AI development lifecycle. This proactive approach ensures that ethical principles are interwoven into the very fabric of AI systems, mitigating security risks from the outset. By delving into these strategies, organizations are equipped not just with defenses but with principled armor, fostering trust in the deployment of AI systems.

In the intricate dance between innovation and responsibility, this chapter spotlights the critical intersection of AI, security, and regulatory compliance. As AI technologies advance, so does the imperative to navigate the legal landscape to ensure adherence to emerging regulations.

Embarking on the exploration of AI's regulatory landscape requires a comprehensive understanding of the global and regional regulations shaping its future. Imagine a tech conglomerate deploying AI on a global scale. The regulatory landscape becomes a dynamic patchwork, with different regions imposing distinct rules. From the General Data Protection Regulation (GDPR) in Europe to evolving guidelines in Asia and North America, organizations must adeptly navigate this terrain. This section illuminates the emerging regulatory constellations that govern AI, guiding organizations through the legal intricacies.

- **Navigating Compliance:** Guiding Organizations Through the Legal Maze

Compliance is not merely a checkbox but a strategic imperative. Organizations need a compass to navigate the complex maze of regulations, encompassing data protection laws, ethical guidelines, and more. Picture an organization employing AI for personalized healthcare. Ensuring compliance involves not only protecting patient data but also aligning with evolving medical ethics. This section delves into actionable steps, emphasizing the proactive measures organizations can adopt to ensure adherence to regulations. By doing so, organizations not only meet legal requirements but also foster a culture of ethical AI deployment.

In the intricate dance between innovation and responsibility, this chapter shines a spotlight on the vital interplay of AI, security, and the ethical considerations that underpin its development. As AI technologies advance, so does the need to address evolving challenges and opportunities while fostering ethical practices.

Embarking on the exploration of AI ethics involves understanding the dynamic nature of the ethical landscape. Imagine an AI-driven social media platform adapting to user behaviors. Ethical considerations extend beyond preventing harm; they delve into fostering transparency, fairness, and accountability. This section scrutinizes the evolving challenges, from bias in algorithms to the ethical implications of AI in healthcare. By considering these nuances, organizations can steer their AI initiatives toward responsible and inclusive innovation.

Just as a ship needs a captain to navigate tumultuous waters, organizations deploying AI benefit from dedicated ethics committees. Picture an e-commerce giant utilizing AI in product recommendations. An AI ethics committee becomes the compass, ensuring that the algorithms align with ethical principles, and avoiding discriminatory practices. This section outlines the formation and function of these committees, emphasizing their pivotal role in promoting ethical AI practices. By integrating ethics committees into their framework, organizations not only adhere to ethical standards but also instill a culture of responsibility in their AI endeavors.

In the evolving tapestry of AI, this section navigates the intricate balance between innovation and responsibility. It places a spotlight on the crucial realm of ensuring ethical AI practices, providing a roadmap for developers and organizations to weave ethics seamlessly into the fabric of AI development.

Defining the ethical foundations of AI involves embracing principles that act as guiding lights. Imagine an AI-powered recruitment tool that employs fairness as a core principle. Here, fairness ensures that the hiring process avoids favoring any group, fostering inclusivity.

This section introduces and explores core ethical principles like fairness, transparency, accountability, and inclusivity. By adhering to these principles, organizations lay the groundwork for AI systems that align with ethical standards.

Addressing bias in AI is akin to uncovering shadows in the data. Picture an AI-driven loan approval system. Bias detection becomes crucial to ensure that decisions aren't influenced by factors like race or gender. This part delves into the challenges of bias in AI and methods for identifying, mitigating, and preventing bias in AI systems. Real-life applications highlight how organizations can proactively address bias to create fair and just AI solutions.

Crafting AI with conscience involves incorporating ethical considerations into the design process. Envision an AI-powered healthcare assistant designed with privacy as a paramount principle. This section explores the importance of ethical AI design, ensuring that considerations like privacy are embedded from the outset. By integrating ethical design practices, organizations create AI systems that not only function effectively but also uphold ethical standards throughout their lifecycle.

Chapter 6 – Data Management for the Future

AI is Chess, Not Checkers!

In the ever-evolving realm of AI, staying ahead is not just an option; it's a necessity. This concluding chapter is a compass for executives navigating the future, providing insights into the latest AI trends and emerging technologies. It's not just about catching up; it's about anticipating what's next.

As AI becomes an integral part of the workforce, understanding the future of work is paramount. This chapter delves into how AI transforms the professional landscape, offering a glimpse into the symbiotic relationship between humans and machines. It's not a replacement; it's a collaboration.

In the race to harness the potential of AI, staying ahead requires strategic finesse. This chapter explores the tactics and mindsets needed to not just participate but lead. It's not about keeping pace; it's about setting it.

Continuous learning and adaptation are the linchpins of success in an AI-driven world. This chapter unwraps the strategies for ongoing growth, ensuring that executives and organizations don't just survive but thrive. It's not about a one-time adaptation; it's about a perpetual evolution.

In the grand finale of this journey, the chapter encapsulates the essence of preparing for the future in an AI-driven landscape. It's not a static endpoint; it's a dynamic process, an ongoing commitment to agility, innovation, and leadership. The future is not a destination; it's a canvas waiting to be painted with the strokes of AI brilliance.

In this chapter, we ventured into the intricate landscape of AI Security and Ethics. Imagine AI as a powerful tool, much like a double-edged sword—it can bring immense benefits, but without careful handling, it poses risks. The first part illuminated the shadows, exploring the myriad risks AI systems face, from data breaches to adversarial attacks. Think of it like protecting your home from potential intruders; AI systems need robust defenses. We then dived into a concept—' ethical by design,' emphasizing the importance of embedding ethical considerations throughout the AI development lifecycle.

The second section took us on a journey through the future landscape of AI Ethics. Consider it as predicting the weather in the ever-changing climate of technology. We discussed the emergence of AI regulations globally and regionally, highlighting the importance of adhering to these guidelines. It's like driving on a road with traffic rules; following them ensures a safer journey. Lastly, we looked at the formation and function of AI ethics committees within organizations. Think of them as guides on this AI journey, ensuring that ethical practices are not just a checkbox but a continuous commitment.

Closing this chapter, we emphasized the significance of addressing AI security risks and upholding ethical practices. It's about building trust in AI systems, complying with regulations, and contributing to the responsible and sustainable development of AI. Just as we navigate through life with a moral compass, organizations, too, must guide AI with principles that stand the test of ethical scrutiny. This chapter equips you with the insights and tools needed to embark on this ethical AI journey, fostering responsible innovation in the ever-evolving world of technology.

Riding the Wave: AI Trends and Emerging Technologies

Welcome to the frontier of AI, where innovation is the norm, and technologies shape the future. In this chapter, we'll take a stroll through the buzzing marketplace of AI, explaining the trends and technologies that are not just shaping today but also pointing to tomorrow.

Current AI Trends: Navigating the Now

Imagine AI trends as the current of a river, always moving, shaping the landscape around it. The current AI trends include:

- **Advancements in Natural Language Processing (NLP):** Think of your virtual assistant understanding your words and context, like a helpful friend comprehending your language.

- **Computer Vision:** Picture cameras not just capture images but interpret and understand them—enabling facial recognition, autonomous vehicles, and more.

- **Reinforcement Learning:** Consider computer learning by trial and error, like a child learning to ride a bike, making mistakes, and getting better with each attempt.

Now, let's peer into the horizon, where the sun of innovation is about to rise. Emerging AI technologies include:

- **Quantum Computing:** Imagine a computer that doesn't think in 0s and 1s but in the quantum realm, handling complex computations much faster than today's computers.

- **Neuromorphic Engineering:** Think of AI systems designed to mimic the human brain's structure and function, creating machines with advanced cognitive capabilities.

- **AI-Powered Robotics:** Envision robots did not just follow pre-programmed instructions but learned and adapted to their environment, becoming more versatile and intelligent.

In this AI landscape, trends are the waves that carry us forward, and emerging technologies are the distant shores where the journey leads. Understanding these currents and horizons is like having a compass in the vast sea of AI possibilities—essential for anyone navigating the tech terrain.

The Future of Work with AI: Embracing a New Era

Welcome to the workplace of tomorrow, where the synergy between humans and AI paints a canvas of innovation and transformation. In this chapter, we'll explore how AI is not just a tool but a collaborator in our professional landscape.

Think of AI as a colleague, not a replacement. It's reshaping the workforce in these ways:

- **Impact on Industries:** Imagine AI optimizing workflows in healthcare, assisting in financial analysis, and driving efficiencies in manufacturing—impacting diverse sectors.

- **Evolution of Job Roles:** Consider job roles evolving. With AI handling routine tasks, humans can focus on creativity, problem-solving, and tasks that require emotional intelligence.

- **Skills for the AI Era:** Picture a workforce equipped with skills like data literacy, adaptability, and collaboration— essential in the era where AI is a team member.

Chapter 7 - The Human and AI Collaboration

The Dance of Innovation

Now, let's dance with the idea of humans and AI working hand in virtual hand:

- **Augmenting Human Capabilities:** Envision AI enhancing human abilities, like a digital assistant amplifying productivity or a robot aiding physical tasks.

- **New Avenues for Innovation:** Picture a scenario where human creativity combines with AI's analytical prowess, sparking innovation in ways neither could achieve alone.

- **Creating Opportunities:** Think of AI not as a competitor but as a co-creator, opening doors to new job roles, industries, and unexplored territories of professional growth.

In this chapter, we're not just witnessing the future of work; we're participants in its creation. The interplay between AI and humans is not a clash but a collaboration—a symphony where each note, whether played by humans or machines, contributes to the melody of progress.

Staying Ahead in the AI Race: A Blueprint for Success

Fasten your seatbelts as we navigate the dynamic landscape of AI, where staying ahead isn't just a strategy; it's a necessity.

In this race, AI isn't just a vehicle; it's the track itself. Here's how:

- **Market Positioning:** Picture AI as a compass guiding business to strategic.

- **Positions in the market:** Those who harness its power effectively gain a competitive edge.

- **Customer Engagement:** Imagine AI as a personalized concierge, enhancing customer experiences. From recommendation systems to chatbots, AI is the secret sauce for unparalleled engagement.

- **Innovation and Agility:** Thriving in the Winds of Change.

Now, let's talk about not just surviving but thriving in the AI race:

- **Cultural Innovation:** Envision a workplace culture where innovation isn't a buzzword but a way of life. AI thrives in environments that encourage experimentation and learning.

- **Agile Responses:** Think of AI as a gust of wind that can propel or impede progress. Agility is the sail that catches that wind, allowing organizations to navigate changes seamlessly.

- **Effective Disruption Response:** Picture a company that doesn't fear disruption but embraces it. AI isn't a storm to weather; it's the wind in the sails of businesses that are ready to adapt.

Adaptive Leadership

In this section, Adaptive Leadership. We're not just spectators watching the AI race; we're crafting strategies to be at the forefront. AI isn't a challenge; it's an opportunity to redefine what it means to lead in a world where innovation is the currency of success.

- **Continuous Learning and Adaptation:** Navigating the Ever-Changing AI Landscape

Strap in for a journey into the heart of the AI storm, where continuous learning isn't just a recommendation; it's a survival strategy.

- **Individual Empowerment:** Imagine AI as a rapid river, and continuous learning as the boat that not only stays afloat but navigates the currents. Lifelong learning is the paddle that propels individuals forward.

  - Key Takeaway: Embrace lifelong learning as you paddle in the AI river; it's not just about staying afloat but reaching new shores.

- **Organizational Evolution:** Think of an organization as an ecosystem. In the AI jungle, only the adaptable survive. Continuous learning isn't a choice; it's the DNA of organizations that thrive.

  - Key Takeaway: For organizations, continuous learning is not a strategy; it's the very fabric that allows adaptation and evolution in the face of AI disruptions.

☐

- **Navigating Turbulence:** Picture AI advancements as a storm. Adaptive leadership is the captain who not only keeps the ship steady but charts a course through uncharted waters.

  - Key Takeaway: Adaptive leaders don't just weather storms; they use the winds of change to set a course for new opportunities.

- **Driving Transformations:** Envision a leader as a gardener of innovation. Adaptive leadership isn't about weathering storms; it's about planting seeds of change and cultivating a garden of continuous improvement.

  - Key Takeaway: Leaders aren't just responding to change; they are architects of transformations, creating a landscape for innovation to bloom.

In the ever-changing AI landscape, learning isn't an event; it's a lifestyle. This chapter isn't just a guide; it's a call to action. By embracing continuous learning and adaptive leadership, individuals and organizations not only survive the AI storm but emerge as architects of the future.

Recap of Key Takeaways:

- **Holistic Impact:** AI is not a mere technology; it's a transformative force touching every aspect of modern business.

- **Executive Leadership**: From strategy to culture, executives play a crucial role in steering the AI ship.

- **Ethics and Security:** Navigating ethical and security dimensions is integral to AI leadership.

- **Measuring Impact:** Continuous measurement of AI impact is vital for sustained success.

- **Closing Thought:** In the world of AI, those who learn, adapt, and lead are the true champions.

In the dynamic landscape of AI, leadership plays a central role in determining the trajectory of organizations and influencing the broader development of AI for societal benefit. Here are the key aspects of the role of AI leadership in shaping the future:

Visionary Leadership:

- **Defining the North Star:** AI leaders are akin to navigators in uncharted waters. They set a visionary course, defining the organization's AI objectives and aligning them with broader societal goals.

- **Innovation as a Guiding Light:** Visionary leaders inspire a culture of innovation. They foster an environment where AI is seen not just as a tool but as a catalyst for transformative ideas and solutions.

Strategic Implementation

- **Integrating AI into Strategy:** AI isn't a standalone initiative; it's woven into the fabric of organizational strategy. Leaders strategically integrate AI, recognizing it as a core element for achieving business goals.

- **Agile Responses to Change**: The AI landscape is dynamic. Leaders adept in strategic agility can quickly respond to technological advancements, market shifts, and changing consumer behaviors, ensuring their organizations stay ahead.

Ethical Responsibility

Guardians of Ethical AI: Leaders bear the responsibility of ensuring that AI applications adhere to ethical standards. This involves making decisions that prioritize fairness, transparency, accountability, and inclusivity in AI systems.

Addressing Bias and Fairness: Leaders actively work to identify and rectify biases in AI algorithms, promoting fairness and equity. They champion AI systems that are designed to benefit all segments of society.

Driving Societal Impact

Contributing to the AI Ecosystem: AI leaders don't operate in isolation. They actively engage with the broader AI ecosystem, collaborating with other leaders, researchers, and policymakers to contribute positively to societal development.

Balancing Profit and Purpose: Leadership isn't just about financial success; it's about balancing profit with purpose. AI leaders strive for a harmonious integration of economic growth with societal well-being.

Closing Perspective

In shaping the future with AI, leaders are not just steering their organizations; they are influencing the very nature and impact of AI on society. The role is multifaceted, requiring a combination of vision, strategy, ethical stewardship, and a commitment to positive societal outcomes. AI leaders, in essence, are architects of a future where technology serves as a force for good.

Encouragement for Executives to Embrace AI Leadership

Dear Visionary Leaders,

As you step into the realm of AI leadership, we extend our encouragement and support for the transformative journey that lies ahead. Here's a heartfelt message as you navigate the possibilities of AI:

- **A World of Opportunities:** AI opens doors to unprecedented possibilities. Embrace the potential for innovation, efficiency, and impact that AI brings to your organization and industry.

The AI landscape is evolving rapidly. Learning moment to continuous learning ensures that you stay at the forefront, leveraging the latest advancements for strategic advantage.

- **Championing Ethics:** As you steer your organization into the AI-driven future, champion ethical leadership. Your commitment to fairness, transparency, and inclusivity sets a standard for responsible AI implementation.

- **Addressing Challenges:** Acknowledge that challenges may arise. Your ethical compass will guide you in addressing issues like bias, ensuring that AI benefits everyone.

- **Fostering Creativity:** Be the catalyst for innovation. Foster a culture where your team sees AI not as a threat but as a powerful tool for creative problem-solving and growth.

- **Agile Leadership:** Lead with agility. In this guide in a dynamic world of AI, your ability to adapt and guide your team through change will be a cornerstone of success.

- **Continuous Voyage:** AI leadership is not about reaching a fixed destination. It's an ongoing voyage of exploration, discovery, and adaptation. Embrace the journey with enthusiasm.

- **Stewardship of Change:** Your role is that of a steward, guiding your organization through the waves of technological change. With each decision, you shape the future.

- **Thank You for Leading:** We express our gratitude for your commitment to AI leadership. Your vision paves the way for organizational success and contributes to the positive evolution of the AI landscape.

Your journey empowers others. By embracing AI leadership principles, you set a powerful example for peers and future leaders, inspiring a collective movement toward a brighter future.

As we bid farewell to this playbook, remember that the future of AI leadership is indeed yours to shape. Your leadership matters, not just for your organization but for the broader impact it can have on the world. Thank you for joining us on this transformative journey.

☐

Chapter 8 - Reflection and Inspiration

Harmony of Actions, Symphony of Impact

In the vast expanse of AI history, we stand at a crossroads where innovation echoes resonate through time. This chapter is more than a mere chronicle; it's an invitation to reflect on the legacy of diverse minds woven into the fabric of AI.

As we delve into historical milestones, we must unveil the silent architects whose brilliance shaped AI. Like the undercurrents shaping a river, these overlooked voices have enriched the expansive landscape of artificial intelligence.

The genuine legacy of innovation lies in the diversity of ideas contributed by minds from various backgrounds. Ada Lovelace's visionary foresight and George Boole's mathematical prowess stand as a testament to the power of diversity in sculpting the foundations of AI.

Inspiring the Next Generation

- **Celebrating Inclusivity:** Reflecting on the journey isn't just about the past; it's a compass for the future. Inclusivity isn't just moral; it's strategic. In Newton's Law, *"An object at rest remains at rest, and an object in motion remains in motion at constant speed and in a straight line unless acted on by an unbalanced force." This indoctrination is my life.* The acceleration of an object depends on the mass of the object and the amount of force applied.

How I Live 1,2,3?

The first step is to Get Up. Approximately, 7,708 deaths happen per day according to, "" The Centre of Disease Control, "CDC", "Publication: Morbidity and Mortality, *date,* Weekly, July 2019.""

If you are blessed to "Wake Up", I suggest the following steps:

- **Step 1:** Get Up!

- **Step 2:** Do Something. Not anything. Something that you can reflect on as positive at day's end. Remember, an object at rest, remains at rest. You must Do Something!

- **Step 3**: Get a result. "An object in motion remains in motion at a constant speed, "UNLESS" acted on by an unbalanced force.

Newtons' Law seeks action to find a reaction, and diverse perspectives amplify impact. In other words, seek advice on your actions. If you are looking for a job and not getting interviews, I suggest a resume writer.

- **Joy in Diversity**: Embracing AI isn't a solitary Endeavor; it's a communal symphony. When human intelligence converges with artificial intelligence, it yields more than technological progress—it's a celebration of human ingenuity. The joy in this diversity becomes a driving force, infusing passion into every line of code and innovation.

The chapter is an ode to reflection and inspiration, affirming that our collective journey in AI is not just about technology but the people shaping it.

As we reflect on the legacy of innovation, let's be inspired to foster inclusivity, celebrate diversity, and continue this symphony of impact. For, in the words of Newton, every action has an equal and opposite reaction, and in the Law of 1, 2, and 3, the reaction is a joy that reverberates through AI's past, present, and future.

Resource Directory

I. Purpose and Scope

Welcome to the "AI from a Black Guy" Resource Directory—a curated compilation of resources designed to empower and support individuals, especially those from underrepresented backgrounds, who are passionate about and engaged in the field of Artificial Intelligence (AI). This section serves as a compass, guiding you through the overarching purpose and comprehensive scope of this invaluable resource.

1. Empowering Diversity in AI

The primary purpose of this Resource Directory is to address the underrepresentation of Black individuals and other marginalized groups in the AI space. By providing a wealth of educational, professional, and community resources, we aim to empower aspiring AI professionals, researchers, and enthusiasts to thrive in a field that benefits immensely from diverse perspectives.

2. Fostering Inclusivity

Inclusivity is at the core of our mission. We have meticulously curated resources that not only offer technical knowledge but also emphasize the importance of diverse voices and experiences in shaping the future of AI. Our goal is to create an inclusive space where everyone, regardless of background, can find the support and tools they need to excel in the AI ecosystem.

3. Supporting Lifelong Learning

The Resource Directory is a dynamic repository that acknowledges the ever-evolving nature of AI. Whether you are a novice exploring the fundamentals or an experienced professional seeking advanced insight, our directory caters to individuals at various stages of their AI journey. It is a gateway to continuous learning and growth.

B. Navigating the Directory

Understanding the layout and organization of the Resource Directory is crucial for maximizing its utility. We have structured the directory with clear categories and sub-sections to facilitate seamless navigation and ensure that you can quickly locate the resources most relevant to your needs.

1. Section Breakdown

Each major section of the directory corresponds to a key aspect of your AI journey, ranging from education and professional development to tools, organizations, and community engagement. Familiarize yourself with these sections to efficiently explore the wealth of resources available.

2. Sub-Sections for Precision

Within each major section, you will find carefully delineated sub-sections. These sub-divisions further refine the content, enabling you to pinpoint resources based on specific criteria such as education level, career stage, or area of interest. Take advantage of these sub-sections to tailor your exploration.

3. Resource Descriptions

Every resource within the directory is accompanied by a concise yet informative description. These descriptions provide insights into the content, applicability, and relevance of each resource. Use them to make informed decisions about which resources align best with your goals.

As you embark on your journey through the "AI from a Black Guy" Resource Directory, we encourage you to embrace the wealth of knowledge, opportunities, and connections it offers. May this directory catalyze your success and contribute to the vibrant tapestry of diversity within the realm of Artificial Intelligence.

II. Educational Resources

A. Online Courses

1. Platforms for AI Education

a. Coursera

Description: Coursera is a leading online learning platform offering a plethora of AI courses from top universities and organizations. It provides a structured learning environment with hands-on projects, ensuring a comprehensive understanding of AI concepts.

- **Key Features:**
  - Diverse course offerings from beginner to advanced levels.
  - Certifications and Specializations in AI and machine learning.
  - Access to instructors and peer interaction through forums.

b. . edX

Description: edX is a platform founded by Harvard and MIT, delivering high-quality AI courses. It offers a mix of free and paid courses, with content developed by renowned institutions and industry experts.

- Key Features:
  - Micro Masters and Professional Certificate programs for specialization.

- o Collaborations with industry leaders for real-world insights.
- o Flexible learning schedules to accommodate diverse learners.

c. Udacity

Description: Udacity provides hands-on AI courses created in collaboration with industry professionals. Its nano degree programs offer project-based learning, providing practical skills for real-world applications.

- o Key Features:
  - o Industry-relevant projects for building a strong portfolio.
  - o Mentorship and personalized feedback for skill development.
  - o Career services to support job placement in the AI industry.

2. Recommended Courses on AI Fundamentals

a. "Introduction to Artificial Intelligence" by Stanford University (Coursera)

Description: Taught by AI pioneer Andrew Ng, this course covers the basics of AI, machine learning, and neural networks. It includes hands-on programming assignments to reinforce theoretical concepts.

o   Key Learning Objectives:
    o   Understanding machine learning algorithms.
    o   Implementing neural networks using programming languages.

b. "Machine Learning" by University of Washington (edX)

Description: This course delves into machine learning concepts, emphasizing practical applications. It explores various algorithms and techniques, offering a solid foundation for AI enthusiasts.

o   Key Learning Objectives:
    o   Applying machine learning algorithms to real-world problems.
    o   Gaining insights into supervised and unsupervised learning.

c. "AI Programming with Python" by Udacity

Description: An introductory course for Python enthusiasts, focusing on AI programming. It covers essential Python libraries for AI development and includes hands-on coding exercises.

o   Key Learning Objectives:
    o   Python programming skills for AI applications.
    o   Building a foundation for advanced AI programming.

B. Books and Reading Materials

1. Essential Reading on Artificial Intelligence

a. Artificial Intelligence: A Modern Approach by Stuart Russell and Peter Norvig

Description: Widely regarded as a comprehensive AI textbook, it covers fundamental concepts, methodologies, and real-world applications. Suitable for both beginners and experienced practitioners.

- o Key Highlights:
  - o In-depth coverage of AI algorithms and problem-solving.
  - o Practical insights into AI research and development.

b. "Life 3.0: Being Human in the Age of Artificial Intelligence" by Max Tegmark

Description: Tegmark explores the societal impact of AI, discussing its potential benefits and risks. It encourages readers to contemplate the ethical and philosophical dimensions of AI.

- o Key Highlights:
  - o Ethical considerations and discussions on the future of AI.
  - o Accessible insights for a broad audience.

2. Diverse Perspectives on AI

a. Race After Technology: Abolitionist Tools for the New Jim Code" by Ruha Benjamin

Description: Benjamin examines the intersection of race and technology, critically analyzing how AI can perpetuate biases. It offers a thought-provoking perspective on the societal implications of AI.

- o Key Highlights:
    - o Exploration of racial bias in AI systems.
    - o Suggestions for addressing bias and promoting equity in technology.

b. "Artificial Unintelligence: How Computers Misunderstand the World" by Meredith Broussard

Description: Broussard challenges the notion that AI is a panacea for all problems. The book provides a critical view of AI's limitations and the importance of understanding its boundaries.

- o Key Highlights:
    - o Examination of AI misconceptions and limitations.
    - o Calls for a nuanced understanding of AI's role in society.

These educational resources aim to equip you with a strong foundation in AI, from theoretical principles to practical applications, while also encouraging a critical examination of AI's societal impact and ethical considerations. Explore these courses and books to embark on a holistic learning journey in the field of Artificial Intelligence.

III. Professional Development

A. Networking Opportunities

1. Conferences and Events

a. NeurIPS (Conference on Neural Information Processing Systems)

Description: NeurIPS is a premier conference that brings together researchers, practitioners, and industry professionals in the field of machine learning and AI. Attendees can explore cutting-edge research, engage in workshops, and network with leading experts.

- o Key Features:
    - o Diverse sessions covering various AI topics.
    - o Opportunities for networking with researchers and industry leaders.
    - o Inclusive and supportive atmosphere.

b. Black in AI Workshop

Description: This workshop, often held in conjunction with major AI conferences, focuses on showcasing the work of Black researchers in AI. It provides a platform for networking, collaboration, and discussions on diversity and inclusion in the AI community.

- o Key Features:
    - o Spotlight on Black voices in AI research.
    - o Networking opportunities specific to underrepresented groups.
    - o Panels addressing diversity and equity in the field.

c. AI Summit

Description: The AI Summit is a global series of conferences that gathers AI professionals, executives, and thought leaders. It offers a platform for sharing insights, discussing AI trends, and building valuable connections.

- o Key Features:
    - o Industry-specific tracks for focused discussions.
    - o Exhibitions showcasing AI innovations.
    - o Networking opportunities with professionals across sectors.

2. Online Forums and Communities

a. AI Village (online community)

Description: AI Village is an online community that provides a space for AI enthusiasts to connect, share knowledge, and collaborate. It encompasses a diverse range of topics, from technical discussions to career advice.

- o Key Features:
    - o Forums for discussing AI research and projects.
    - o Networking threads for connecting with peers.
    - o Mentorship opportunities within the community.

b. Black in AI Community

Description: The Black in AI Community is a platform dedicated to fostering collaboration and support among Black professionals and researchers in AI. It includes forums, webinars, and networking events designed to create a sense of community within the AI landscape.

- o Key Features:
    - o Networking opportunities for Black professionals.
    - o Resources and discussions on diversity in AI.
    - o Collaboration on research and projects.

c. Stack Overflow - AI Section

Description: Stack Overflow is a widely used platform for asking and answering programming-related questions. The AI section is a hub for technical discussions, problem-solving, and connecting with AI practitioners globally.

- o Key Features:
    - o Q&A format for technical problem-solving.
    - o Discussion threads on AI algorithms and tools.
    - o Opportunity to connect with AI professionals.

B. Mentorship Programs

1. Connecting with Industry Leaders

a. AI Mentors Program

Description: The AI Mentors Program pairs aspiring AI professionals with experienced mentors in the field. It provides a structured mentorship framework, allowing mentees to gain insights, guidance, and personalized advice from seasoned industry leaders.

- Key Features:
    - One-on-one mentorship sessions.
    - Networking events for mentees to connect.
    - Access to industry-specific insights and career advice.

b. Industry-Specific Mentorship Programs

Description: Many industries and organizations offer mentorship programs tailored to individuals interested in AI. These programs connect mentees with mentors who have expertise in a specific sector, fostering industry-specific knowledge and connections.

- Key Features:
    - Mentorship aligned with career goals and industry interests.
    - Networking opportunities within the chosen sector.
    - Guidance on navigating the intersection of AI and specific industries.

2. Support Networks for Black Professionals in AI

a. Blacks in Technology (BIT)

Description: Blacks in Technology is a community-driven organization focused on promoting the inclusion of Black professionals in the tech industry, including AI. It offers networking events, mentorship programs, and a supportive community for Black individuals pursuing careers in technology.

- o Key Features:
    - o Networking opportunities and events.
    - o Mentorship programs tailored for Black professionals.
    - o Resources and support for career development.

b. National Society of Black Engineers (NSBE)

Description: NSBE is an organization dedicated to supporting Black engineers and promoting diversity in STEM fields. It provides networking opportunities, mentorship programs, and resources to empower Black professionals in AI and related disciplines.

- o Key Features:
    - o Annual conferences and events for networking.
    - o Mentorship initiatives connecting students and professionals.
    - o Scholarships and career development resources.

Professional development in AI is not only about acquiring technical skills but also about building a strong network and seeking guidance from experienced mentors. Explore these networking opportunities and mentorship programs to enhance your professional journey and contribute to a more diverse and inclusive AI community.

IV. Funding and Scholarships

A. Scholarships for AI Studies

1. Opportunities for Underrepresented Groups

a. AI Diversity Scholarship

Description: The AI Diversity Scholarship is dedicated to supporting underrepresented groups, including Black individuals, pursuing studies in AI. It aims to foster diversity in the field by providing financial assistance to students committed to making a meaningful impact.

- o Key Features:
  - o Financial support for tuition and related expenses.
  - o Opportunities for mentorship and networking.
  - o Emphasis on supporting students from diverse backgrounds.

b. NSF Graduate Research Fellowship Program

Description: The National Science Foundation (NSF) offers the Graduate Research Fellowship Program, which includes a focus on increasing diversity in STEM fields, including AI. It provides financial support to graduate students conducting research in areas relevant to AI.

- o Key Features:
  - o Three years of financial support, including stipends.
  - o Opportunities for international research experiences.
  - o Emphasis on supporting a diverse and inclusive research community.

c. Google AI Residency Program

Description: Google's AI Residency Program is designed to provide aspiring researchers with hands-on experience in AI and machine learning. The program includes a stipend, and Google is committed to fostering diversity by encouraging individuals from underrepresented backgrounds to apply.

- o Key Features:
    - o Stipend and support for research projects.
    - o Collaboration with leading researchers at Google.
    - o Focus on increasing diversity in AI research.

2. Financial Aid for AI Research Projects

a. OpenAI Scholarship

Description: The OpenAI Scholarship aims to support individuals interested in pursuing research in artificial general intelligence (AGI). It provides financial aid to cover living expenses and resources necessary for contributing to AGI safety and policy research.

- o Key Features:
    - o Financial support for living expenses during the research period.
    - o Mentorship and guidance from OpenAI researchers.
    - o Opportunity to make meaningful contributions to AGI research.

b. Microsoft AI for Accessibility Grants

Description: Microsoft's AI for Accessibility program offers grants to individuals and organizations working on projects that leverage AI to empower people with disabilities. The program supports a wide range of AI-driven initiatives to foster inclusivity.

- o Key Features:
    - o Grants for AI projects focused on accessibility.
    - o Support for both individuals and organizations.
    - o Commitment to promoting diversity and inclusion in technology.

B. Grant Opportunities

1. Funding Initiatives for AI Startups

a. AI Impact Grant by NVIDIA

Description: NVIDIA's AI Impact Grant is designed to support startups that are leveraging AI for positive social and environmental impact. The grant provides financial support, technical assistance, and access to NVIDIA's expertise and resources.

- o Key Features:
    - o Funding for AI startups addressing societal challenges.
    - o Technical support and resources from NVIDIA.
    - o Opportunities for collaboration and networking.

b. Google Cloud for Startups - Black Founders Fund

Description: Google Cloud for Startups offers the Black Founders Fund to support Black-led startups, including those working on AI and machine learning projects. The fund provides financial assistance, cloud credits, and access to Google's network.

- o Key Features:
    - o Funding for Black-led startups utilizing AI technologies.
    - o Google Cloud credits and technical support.
    - o Mentorship and networking opportunities.

2. Grants Supporting Diversity in AI Research

a. Partnership on AI (PAI) Funding

Description: The Partnership on AI (PAI) offers funding opportunities to organizations and researchers working on projects that align with PAI's mission to ensure AI benefits all of humanity. They actively seek projects that promote diversity, inclusion, and ethical considerations in AI development.

- o Key Features:
    - o Funding for AI research projects aligned with PAI's goals.
    - o Emphasis on diversity, inclusion, and ethical AI.
    - o Collaboration opportunities with PAI's partner organizations.

b. DARPA Artificial Intelligence Exploration (AIE) Program

Description: The Defense Advanced Research Projects Agency (DARPA) offers the AIE Program to support innovative and high-risk AI research. While not explicitly focused on diversity, DARPA encourages a diverse pool of researchers to contribute to cutting-edge AI advancements.

- o Key Features:
    - o Funding for innovative and high-impact AI research.
    - o Encouragement for diversity in research teams.
    - o Emphasis on transformative and breakthrough AI technologies.

Navigating the landscape of funding and scholarships in AI can be a pivotal step in advancing your studies or research projects. Explore these opportunities to access financial support, mentorship, and resources that align with your goals, while contributing to the diversity and inclusivity of the AI community.

V. Tools and Platforms

A. AI Development Tools

1. Software and Frameworks

a. TensorFlow

Description: Developed by Google, TensorFlow is an open-source machine learning framework widely used for building and deploying AI models. It offers a comprehensive ecosystem, including tools for neural network development, natural language processing, and computer vision.

- Key Features:
    - Flexibility for creating a range of machine learning models.
    - Large community and extensive documentation.
    - Support for both beginners and advanced users.

b. PyTorch

Description: PyTorch is a popular open-source deep learning framework known for its dynamic computational graph, making it suitable for research and experimentation. It is widely used for tasks such as image classification, natural language processing, and reinforcement learning.

- Key Features:
    - Dynamic computation for more intuitive model development.
    - Strong support for research and experimentation.
    - Growing ecosystem and active community.

c. Scikit-learn

Description: Scikit-learn is a simple and efficient tool for data analysis and modeling. It provides a variety of machine learning algorithms and tools for tasks such as classification, regression, clustering, and dimensionality reduction.

- o Key Features:
    - o User-friendly interface for quick implementation.
    - o An extensive set of algorithms for diverse machine learning tasks.
    - o Seamless integration with other data science libraries.

2. Platforms for Collaborative AI Projects

a. GitHub

Description: GitHub is a widely used platform for version control and collaborative software development. It is an essential tool for AI practitioners, enabling them to collaborate on code, manage projects, and contribute to open-source AI initiatives.

- o Key Features:
    - o Version control for tracking code changes.
    - o Collaboration features such as pull requests and issues.
    - o Hosting repositories for sharing and collaborating on projects.

b. Kaggle

Description: Kaggle is a platform that hosts data science competitions and provides datasets for exploration. It offers a collaborative environment where data scientists and AI practitioners can share code, kernels, and insights, fostering a sense of community.

- o Key Features:
  - o Access to diverse datasets for AI projects.
  - o Collaboration with a global community of data scientists.
  - o Competitions to test and enhance AI skills.

c. Colab by Google

Description: Google Colab is a cloud-based platform that provides free access to GPU resources, making it an excellent choice for AI development. It allows users to create and share Jupyter notebooks, facilitating collaborative coding and experimentation.

- o Key Features:
  - o Free access to GPU resources for accelerated computations.
  - o Integration with Google Drive for easy sharing and collaboration.
  - o Pre-installed libraries for machine learning and data analysis.

B. Data Sets for AI Projects

1. Diverse and Inclusive Data Sets

a. ImageNet

Description: ImageNet is a large-scale dataset with millions of labeled images across thousands of categories. It is commonly used for training and benchmarking computer vision models and promotes diversity in image classification tasks.

- o Key Features:
    - o A large and diverse collection of images.
    - o Widely adopted for computer vision research.
    - o Helps in developing models with broad applicability.

b. COCO (Common Objects in Context) Dataset

Description: The COCO dataset consists of images with complex scenes and a diverse set of objects. It includes annotations for object detection, segmentation, and captioning tasks, making it valuable for developing AI models with contextual understanding.

- o Key Features:
    - o Rich annotations for various computer vision tasks.
    - o Emphasis on context and real-world scenes.
    - o Widely used for benchmarking object detection algorithms.

2. Ethical Data Collection Resources

a. AI Fairness 360 Toolkit

Description: Developed by IBM, the AI Fairness 360 Toolkit is an open-source library that helps in detecting and mitigating biases in machine learning models. It provides tools and algorithms to assess and address fairness concerns in AI systems.

- o Key Features:
    - o Tools for measuring and mitigating bias in datasets.
    - o Addresses fairness concerns in AI models.
    - o Supports various machine learning frameworks.

b. Datasheets for Datasets (D4D)

Description: D4D is an initiative that promotes transparency and ethical considerations in data collection. It encourages the creation of datasheets for datasets, providing a structured way to document important aspects such as the purpose, composition, and potential biases of a dataset.

- o Key Features:
    - o Framework for documenting key aspects of datasets.
    - o Promotes transparency and ethical data practices.
    - o Helps users understand and evaluate dataset biases.

c. Data Ethics Canvas

Description: The Data Ethics Canvas is a practical tool for individuals and teams involved in data-related projects. It provides a structured framework for discussing and addressing ethical considerations throughout the data lifecycle, including data collection.

o Key Features:
   o Canvas format for visualizing ethical considerations.
   o Facilitates discussions on potential ethical issues.
   o Guides users in making ethical decisions during data collection.

As you embark on AI projects, these tools and platforms are invaluable resources for development, collaboration, and ethical data practices. Utilize them to enhance the efficiency and inclusivity of your AI initiatives, while keeping ethical considerations at the forefront of your work.

VI. Organizations and Initiatives

A. Diversity and Inclusion Initiatives

1. Organizations Focused on Inclusivity in Tech

a. AnitaB.org

Description: AnitaB.org is a global nonprofit organization dedicated to advancing women in technology. Through events, programs, and initiatives, AnitaB.org strives to create a more inclusive and diverse tech industry. The organization hosts the Grace Hopper Celebration, the world's largest gathering of women technologists.

- o Key Features:
    - o Advocacy for gender diversity in technology.
    - o Programs to support women in tech careers.
    - o Community-building events and networking opportunities.

b. Techqueria

Description: Techqueria is a nonprofit that serves the largest community of Latinx professionals in the tech industry. It focuses on providing resources, mentorship, and networking opportunities to empower Latinx individuals pursuing careers in technology.

- o Key Features:
    - o Support and networking for Latinx professionals.
    - o Career development and mentorship programs.
    - o Community events foster collaboration and inclusivity.

a. AI4ALL

Description: AI4ALL is a nonprofit organization working to increase diversity and inclusion in artificial intelligence. The organization offers education programs, mentorship, and community-building initiatives to underrepresented groups, including women and individuals from marginalized communities.

- o Key Features:
    - o Educational programs for high school students.
    - o Mentoring and support for underrepresented individuals.
    - o Advocacy for diversity in AI education and research.

b. Women in Machine Learning (WiML)

Description: Women in Machine Learning (WiML) is a community that focuses on supporting and promoting women in the field of machine learning. It organizes workshops, conferences, and networking events to create opportunities for women to excel in machine learning research and applications.

- o Key Features:
    - o Annual workshops and events for women in machine learning.
    - o Networking opportunities and mentorship programs.
    - o Contributions to advancing women's representation in AI research.

B. Advocacy Groups

1. Organizations Addressing Ethical AI Concerns

a. Algorithmic Justice League (AJL)

Description: The Algorithmic Justice League, founded by Joy Buolamwini, focuses on addressing bias and promoting equity in algorithmic systems. AJL engages in research, advocacy, and outreach to highlight the ethical implications of AI and hold organizations accountable for biased technologies.

- o Key Features:
    - o Research on bias in facial recognition and AI systems.
    - o Advocacy for equitable AI practices and policies.
    - o Educational initiatives to raise awareness about algorithmic bias.

a. Center for Humane Technology

Description: The Center for Humane Technology is an organization advocating for the ethical use of technology to prioritize human well-being. Led by former tech insiders, the center works to address issues such as addiction, misinformation, and the impact of technology on mental health.

- o Key Features:
    - o Research on the impact of technology on society.
    - o Advocacy for ethical design and responsible tech practices.
    - o Educational efforts to promote digital well-being.

2. Platforms for AI Policy Advocacy

a. AI Now Institute

Description: The AI Now Institute is dedicated to studying and addressing the social implications of artificial intelligence. As a research institute, it conducts interdisciplinary research, advocates for policy changes, and collaborates with policymakers to ensure the responsible development and deployment of AI technologies.

- o Key Features:
  - o Research on the societal impacts of AI technologies.
  - o Policy recommendations and advocacy for responsible AI.
  - o Collaboration with policymakers and organizations.

b. Electronic Frontier Foundation (EFF)

Description: The Electronic Frontier Foundation is a leading organization advocating for digital rights and civil liberties in the digital world. While not AI-specific, EFF actively engages in policy discussions related to AI, surveillance, and privacy, aiming to protect individuals' rights in the era of advanced technologies.

- o Key Features:
  - o Advocacy for privacy rights in the digital age.
  - o Policy initiatives addressing AI and surveillance.
  - o Legal support and defense of civil liberties in technology.

These organizations and initiatives play a crucial role in promoting diversity, inclusion, and ethical considerations in the tech and AI industries. Engaging with these groups can provide valuable resources, networking opportunities, and advocacy for creating a more equitable and responsible technological landscape.

VII. Career Resources

A. Job Portals

1. Platforms for AI Job Opportunities

a. LinkedIn

Description: LinkedIn is a widely used professional networking platform that features job postings across various industries, including AI. AI professionals can leverage LinkedIn to connect with industry peers, follow relevant companies, and discover job opportunities tailored to their expertise.

- o Key Features:
    - o Job postings from a diverse range of companies.
    - o Networking opportunities with AI professionals.
    - o Industry insights and updates on AI trends.

b. Glassdoor

Description: Glassdoor is a platform that provides job listings, company reviews, and salary information. AI professionals can explore job opportunities, research company cultures, and gain insights into salary expectations within the industry.

- o Key Features:
    - o Company reviews for evaluating workplace culture.
    - o Salary insights for informed negotiations.
    - o Job alerts for personalized job recommendations.

c. AI Jobs (ai-jobs.net)

Description: AI Jobs is a dedicated job portal specifically focused on AI and machine learning opportunities. It aggregates AI job listings from various sources, making it a convenient platform for professionals seeking roles in the field.

o   Key Features:
   o   Curated job listings in AI and machine learning.
   o   User-friendly interface for easy job exploration.
   o   Regularly updated with new AI job opportunities.

2. Companies Emphasizing Diversity in Hiring

a. Intel Corporation

Description: Intel is committed to diversity and inclusion in its workforce. The company actively seeks to create an inclusive environment and encourages applicants from diverse backgrounds, including underrepresented groups in the tech industry.

o   Key Features:
   o   Diversity and inclusion initiatives and programs.
   o   Support for employees from various backgrounds.
   o   Opportunities for career growth and development.

b. Microsoft

Description: Microsoft is dedicated to fostering a diverse and inclusive workplace. The company actively recruits talent from different backgrounds and supports initiatives to promote diversity in the tech industry. Microsoft emphasizes creating an inclusive culture where all employees can thrive.

- o Key Features:
    - o Diversity and inclusion programs and initiatives.
    - o Employee resource groups for networking and support.
    - o Inclusive policies and practices in hiring.

c. IBM

Description: IBM prioritizes diversity and inclusion in its workforce, recognizing the value of varied perspectives in driving innovation. The company actively supports initiatives to promote diversity in technology and offers programs for professional development and advancement.

- o Key Features:
    - o Inclusive hiring practices and policies.
    - o Diversity and inclusion programs and networks.
    - o Opportunities for skill development and career growth.

B. Resume Building and Interview Tips

1. Guidance for Crafting an AI-Centric Resume

a. Highlight Technical Skills:

Emphasize your proficiency in AI-related tools, programming languages, and frameworks. Clearly articulate your experience with machine learning algorithms, data analysis, and any specific AI projects you've worked on.

b. Showcase Projects:

Create a dedicated section for AI projects you've completed. Detail the problem statements, methodologies employed, and the impact of the projects. Include any open-source contributions or collaborations with other AI professionals.

c. Quantify Achievements:

Use quantifiable metrics to showcase the impact of your work. Highlight how your contributions led to improved efficiency, accuracy, or other measurable outcomes. Numbers and results can make your resume stand out.

d. Tailor to Job Descriptions:

Customize your resume for each job application by aligning your skills and experiences with the specific requirements outlined in the job description. This ensures that your resume is tailored to the needs of each employer.

2. Strategies for Successful AI Job Interviews

a. Brush Up on Fundamentals:

Be prepared to discuss foundational concepts in AI, machine learning, and data science. Review key algorithms, techniques, and frameworks. Interviewers may ask technical questions to assess your depth of understanding.

b. Demonstrate Problem-Solving Skills:

Expect coding or problem-solving exercises that assess your ability to apply AI concepts to real-world scenarios. Practice coding challenges and algorithmic problem-solving to sharpen your skills.

c. Communicate Clearly:

Clearly articulate your thoughts and reasoning during technical discussions. Interviewers appreciate candidates who can effectively communicate complex ideas. Practice explaining your approach to problem-solving.

d. Showcase Collaboration Skills:

Emphasize your ability to work in collaborative environments. Discuss past experiences where you collaborated with cross-functional teams, communicated findings effectively, and contributed to the success of a project.

e. Stay Informed About Industry Trends:

Keep yourself updated on the latest trends and advancements in AI. Interviewers may ask about your awareness of current industry developments, so staying informed demonstrates your commitment to continuous learning.

As you navigate your AI career, these resources can serve as valuable tools to explore job opportunities, enhance your resume, and prepare for successful interviews.

VIII. Community Engagement

A. AI Meetups and Events

1. Local and Virtual Gatherings

a. Meetup.com

Description: Meetup.com is a platform that facilitates the creation and discovery of local and virtual events, including AI meetups. AI professionals can find or organize events in their area to connect with like-minded individuals, share knowledge, and network.

- o Key Features:
    - o Search for local AI meetups and events.
    - o Join virtual gatherings to connect globally.
    - o Organize and promote AI-related events.

b. Eventbrite

Description: Eventbrite is a platform for discovering and organizing events. AI professionals can explore local and virtual AI meetups, workshops, and conferences. Organizers can use Eventbrite to create and manage events, reaching a broader audience.

- o Key Features:
    - o Discover and register for AI events.
    - o Host and promote AI-related gatherings.
    - o Access a diverse range of AI-focused events.

c. AI Conferences and Summits

Description: Attend major AI conferences and summits, both local and global. Events like NeurIPS, CVPR, and AI conferences by industry leaders provide opportunities to learn about cutting-edge research, network with professionals, and engage in discussions shaping the future of AI.

- o Key Features:
    - o Exposure to the latest AI research and trends.
    - o Networking opportunities with industry experts.
    - o Participation in workshops and discussions.

2. Creating and Hosting AI Events

a. Meetup Organizer

Description: Become a meetup organizer on platforms like Meetup.com to create and host AI events in your local community or virtually. Organizing events allows you to bring together AI enthusiasts, share knowledge, and build a community around common interests.

- o Key Features:
    - o Flexibility to organize events based on interests.
    - o Building a local AI community.
    - o Networking with participants and guest speakers.

b. Online Webinars and Workshops

Description: Host online webinars and workshops on platforms like Zoom or Microsoft Teams. This allows you to share your expertise, invite guest speakers, and engage with a global audience interested in AI topics. Platforms like Crowdcast and Hopin offer features for interactive virtual events.

- o Key Features:
    - o Reach a broader, global audience.
    - o Interactive sessions with Q&A and discussions.
    - o Opportunity to collaborate with other professionals.

B. Social Media and Online Platforms

1. Building an Online Presence in the AI Community

a. LinkedIn

Description: Build a professional profile on LinkedIn to showcase your expertise in AI. Share articles, insights, and updates related to AI. Connect with professionals, join AI groups, and participate in discussions to expand your network and visibility in the AI community.

- o Key Features:
    - o Professional networking opportunities.
    - o Showcase AI-related achievements and projects.
    - o Engage with the broader AI community.

b. Twitter

Description: Create a Twitter account to stay updated on AI trends and participate in conversations using relevant hashtags. Follow AI researchers, professionals, and organizations. Tweet about your AI projects, share interesting articles and engage in discussions to contribute to the AI community.

- o Key Features:
    - o Real-time updates on AI news and discussions.
    - o Hashtags for participating in AI-related conversations.
    - o Networking with professionals and researchers.

c. GitHub

Description: Establish a presence on GitHub to showcase your AI projects, contribute to open-source initiatives, and collaborate with other developers. GitHub serves as a platform for sharing code, collaborating on AI projects, and building a portfolio of your work in the AI field.

- o Key Features:
    - o Share and collaborate on AI projects.
    - o Contribute to open-source AI initiatives.
    - o Showcase coding skills and project contributions.

2. Participating in AI Discussions

a. Reddit (r/MachineLearning)

Description: Join the machine learning community on Reddit to participate in discussions, ask questions, and share your knowledge. Subreddits like r/MachineLearning provide a platform for engaging with a diverse group of AI enthusiasts, researchers, and professionals.

- o Key Features:
    - o Discussions on a wide range of AI topics.
    - o Q&A sessions and knowledge sharing.
    - o Networking with AI enthusiasts and professionals.

b. AI Communities on Slack and Discord

Description: Join AI-focused communities on platforms like Slack and Discord. Many organizations and interest groups have dedicated channels for AI discussions, networking, and collaboration. Engage with community members, ask questions, and contribute to the collective knowledge base.

o   Key Features:
- o   Real-time communication with AI professionals.
- o   Specialized channels for specific AI topics.
- o   Networking and collaboration opportunities.

c. AI Blogs and Forums

Description: Explore and contribute to AI blogs and forums where professionals share insights, research findings, and experiences. Platforms like Towards Data Science on Medium, AI Stack Exchange, and AI Forum provide spaces for in-depth discussions and knowledge exchange.

o   Key Features:
- o   Read and contribute to AI-related articles.
- o   Q&A forums for problem-solving and discussions.
- o   Networking with AI professionals and researchers.

Engaging with the AI community through meetups, events, social media, and online platforms is essential for staying informed, building connections, and contributing to the growth of the AI field. Active participation allows you to share knowledge, learn from others, and establish a strong presence in the AI community.

IX. Wellness and Support

A. Mental Health Resources

1. Coping with Challenges in the AI Field

a. Therapy and Counseling Services

Description: Seeking professional therapy or counseling services can provide valuable support for coping with challenges in the AI field. Therapists with expertise in stress management, burnout, and work-related issues can offer guidance and coping strategies.

- o Key Features:
    - o Confidential and personalized counseling sessions.
    - o Strategies for managing stress and work-related challenges.
    - o Tailored support for individuals in the AI field.

b. Employee Assistance Programs (EAP)

Description: Many companies offer Employee Assistance Programs as part of their benefits package. EAPs provide confidential counseling services and resources to employees dealing with personal or work-related challenges, including those specific to the AI industry.

- o Key Features:
    - o Access to confidential counseling services.
    - o Referrals to mental health professionals.
    - o Resources for managing stress and well-being.

c. Mindfulness and Meditation

Description: Incorporating mindfulness and meditation practices into your routine can help alleviate stress and improve mental well-being. Mindfulness apps, guided meditations, and mindful breathing exercises can be effective tools for managing the pressures of the AI field.

- o Key Features:
    - o Apps offering guided mindfulness sessions.
    - o Breathing exercises for stress reduction.
    - o Techniques for promoting mental clarity.

2. Supportive Communities for Mental Well-being

a. AI Mental Health Support Groups

Description: Joining mental health support groups specifically tailored for individuals in the AI field provides a safe space to share experiences, challenges, and coping strategies. Online forums, group discussions, and peer support can foster a sense of community.

- o Key Features:
    - o Peer support from individuals in the AI community.
    - o Shared experiences and coping strategies.
    - o Anonymity and confidentiality in online forums.

b. Professional Networking with Wellness Focus

Description: Attend networking events and conferences that focus on both professional development and well-being. These events often include sessions on stress management, work-life balance, and mental health in the AI industry, fostering a holistic approach to career growth.

- o Key Features:
    - o Networking opportunities with a focus on well-being.
    - o Educational sessions on mental health in the AI field.
    - o Connection with like-minded professionals.

c. Online Mental Health Platforms

Description: Explore online platforms dedicated to mental health and well-being. Apps and websites offer resources such as articles, forums, and virtual support groups addressing mental health challenges in the tech and AI industries.

- o Key Features:
    - o Access to articles and resources on mental health.
    - o Virtual support groups and forums.
    - o Anonymity and flexibility in online platforms.

B. Work-Life Balance Tips

1. Strategies for Maintaining Balance in AI Careers

a. Set Clear Boundaries

Clearly define work hours and non-work hours to establish a boundary between professional and personal life. Communicate these boundaries to colleagues and adhere to them to promote a healthier work-life balance.

b. Prioritize Self-Care

Make self-care a priority by scheduling regular breaks, exercise, and moments of relaxation. Prioritizing self-care contributes to overall well-being and helps manage stress in the demanding AI industry.

c. Delegate and Collaborate

Delegate tasks when possible and collaborate with team members to share the workload. Effective teamwork can reduce individual stress and contribute to a more balanced workload.

2. Creating Healthy Habits in a High-Tech Environment

a. Screen Time Management

Set limits on screen time to reduce eye strain and promote a healthy balance between work and leisure. Incorporate breaks away from screens to rest your eyes and focus on non-digital activities.

b. Regular Physical Activity

Integrate regular physical activity into your routine to counteract the sedentary nature of many AI-related tasks. Exercise has proven benefits for both physical and mental well-being.

c. Mindful Technology Use

Practice mindful use of technology by setting specific times for checking emails and messages. Avoiding constant connectivity can reduce stress and contribute to a healthier relationship with technology.

Maintaining wellness and achieving a healthy work-life balance is crucial in the fast-paced and demanding field of AI. By accessing mental health resources, participating in supportive communities, and implementing work-life balance strategies, individuals can foster a more sustainable and fulfilling career in the AI industry.

X. Conclusion

A. Acknowledgments and Thanks

As we conclude this journey through "AI from a Black Guy," we extend our heartfelt acknowledgments and thanks to those who have contributed to the realization of this resource directory. It takes a collective effort to weave together the tapestry of knowledge and insights, and we are grateful for the support and collaboration of individuals and organizations.

Acknowledgments:

Nathan D. Cruise, our editor, and Director at Wofford Excellerate Group, for his meticulous attention to detail and dedication to refining the content.

We express our gratitude to the vibrant AI community, readers, and supporters who have engaged with this project. Your enthusiasm and commitment to advancing the field of artificial intelligence inspire us to continue pushing the boundaries of knowledge and innovation.

B. Encouragement for Ongoing Learning and Growth

As the field of artificial intelligence continues to evolve, we encourage every reader to embrace a mindset of ongoing learning and growth. The landscape of AI is dynamic, presenting new challenges and opportunities. Whether you are a seasoned professional or just beginning your journey in AI, the pursuit of knowledge and the commitment to personal and professional growth are the keys to staying relevant and making a lasting impact.

- o Key Takeaways:

- Curiosity and Exploration: Embrace curiosity as a driving force for exploration. The AI field thrives on innovation, and your inquisitiveness can lead to groundbreaking discoveries.
- Continuous Learning: Commit to a lifelong journey of continuous learning. Stay updated on emerging technologies, methodologies, and best practices to remain at the forefront of the AI landscape.
- Community Engagement: Actively engage with the AI community. Networking, participating in discussions, and collaborating with peers can foster collective intelligence and open doors to new possibilities.
- Inclusivity and Diversity: Champion inclusivity and diversity in AI. Diverse perspectives fuel creativity and drive innovation. Encourage and support initiatives that promote equity in the AI workforce.
- Wellness and Balance: Prioritize your well-being and maintain a healthy work-life balance. A sustainable and fulfilling career in AI requires a holistic approach that encompasses mental health, self-care, and a supportive community.

As you navigate the ever-expanding horizons of artificial intelligence, remember that your unique experiences and contributions play a vital role in shaping the future of technology. May this resource directory serve as a compass, guiding you on your path of exploration, learning, and transformative impact.

Thank you for being part of the "AI from a Black Guy" journey. The future of AI is in the hands of diverse and dynamic minds like yours. Keep learning, keep growing, and keep shaping the future of artificial intelligence.

This AI resource directory combines a spectrum of tools and platforms, showcasing the field's diversity of applications and innovations. Whether you're a developer, a business exploring AI solutions, or an enthusiast eager to learn and collaborate, these resources offer a rich tapestry of possibilities in artificial intelligence. Explore them and embark on your AI journey today!

Appendix

Appendix A: Glossary

This section provides a comprehensive glossary of key terms and concepts throughout the book, offering readers a quick reference to enhance their understanding.

AI (Artificial Intelligence): Human AI simulation. (Page 12)

AI Chip: Hardware designed for AI training. (Page 26)

AI Ethics: Ethical principles in AI development. (Page 42)

AI for Good: AI applications for societal impact. (Page 31)

AI Leadership Role: AI's role in leadership. (Page 55)

AI Model Deployment: Real-world applications. (Page 77)

Algorithm: Set of rules for specific tasks. (Page 18)

Algorithmic Fairness: Non-discrimination algorithms. (Page 47)

Algorithmic Trading: Automated trading. (Page 29)

Big Data: Large and complex data sets. (Page 27)

Bias: Systematic errors in AI models. (Page 43)

Chatbot: Program simulating conversation with users. (Page 22)

Cognitive Computing: Human AI simulation. (Page 23)

Collaboration Unveiled: Exploring AI collaboration. (Page 58)

Computer Vision: AI interpreting visual information. (Page 24)

Continuous AI Learning: Ongoing AI model learning. (Page 53)

Crafting Your AI Strategy: Developing AI strategies. (Page 63)

Data as an Asset: Leveraging data in AI. (Page 61)

Data Collection, Quality, and Management: (Page 69)

Data Mining: Discovering patterns in large datasets. (Page 71)

Jeffrey E. Wofford

Jeffrey Wofford, CEO, of Wofford Excellerate Group
(https://www.woffordexcel.com) is a seasoned AI strategist and
technologist passionate about leveraging cutting-edge technologies
to drive innovation and solve complex challenges. With a
background in computer science and a keen interest in artificial
intelligence, Jeffrey has been at the forefront of developing
transformative AI solutions.

As the Author of this book, Jeffrey brings a wealth of experience in
AI project management, technology implementation, and strategic
leadership. He has played a pivotal role in shaping the narrative of
AI adoption, emphasizing the ethical considerations and societal
impact of emerging technologies.

Jeffrey's commitment to fostering collaboration and inclusivity in the
AI community is evident in his work with various organizations and
initiatives. His contributions extend beyond the technical realm,
encompassing a holistic approach to AI that prioritizes ethical
practices, diversity, and positive societal outcomes.

With a vision for a future where AI contributes to the betterment of
humanity, Jeffrey Wofford continues to be a thought leader and
advocate for responsible AI.

Jeffrey E. Wofford is the CEO of Wofford Consulting Excellerate
Group, Sr. Author, and Publishing Company of "AI from a Black
Guy". an AI Consulting firm focused on AI Diversity and Inclusion
of Ethical AI and the Black and Minority communities.

THE END

Made in the USA
Las Vegas, NV
21 February 2024

86000643R00095